JEKYLL HYDES AGAIN!

A Screwball Musical

by

Jack Sharkey & Dave Reiser

SAMUEL FRENCH, INC.

45 WEST 25TH STREET   NEW YORK 10010

7623 SUNSET BOULEVARD HOLLYWOOD 90046

LONDON   TORONTO

MUSIC—IMPORTANT

Music for this production is available, on a rental and deposit basis.

Rental for use of the music is $10.00 for each performance. We can lend you a piano/vocal score for a period of eight weeks, on receipt of the following:

1. Number of performances and exact performance dates.
2. Rental in full on the music for the entire production.
3. Deposit of $25.00, which is refunded on return to us of the material in good condition immediately after your production. Plus first-class postage and handling charge of $2.50.

We cannot fill any order for music unless it is accompanied by remittance as above, as all rental material is handled on a strictly c.o.d. basis.

CAST OF CHARACTERS

JUNIOR JEKYLL [HYDE] . . . . . . a kindly [rotten] doctor [fiend]
LALA . . . . a free-lance lab assistant
THADDEUS GRUMBY . . . . the neighborhood do-gooder
GRETCHEN GRUMBY . . . . Thaddeus's downhearted daughter
PARADISE PLOTKIN . . . . a world-weary saloon-singer

SUPPORTING PLAYERS

BARTENDER/POLICEMAN [dual role for one player]
FEMALE SINGERS #1 AND #2
MALE SINGERS #1 AND #2
[If you like, you may have MALE/FEMALE SINGERS by the dozens; the listing above is the *minimum* required.]

ACT ONE
London, in the mid-1800s

ACT TWO
The following day

This Play Has Been
Dedicated
to
ROBERT LOUIS STEVENSON
(who will probably turn over in his grave)

[NOTE: Those groups wishing to do this show in three acts will find a mid-break in Act One of the script specified for this purpose. The Entr'Acte Music for the additional act will be the same as for Act Two.]

JEKYLL HYDES AGAIN!

MUSICAL NUMBERS

OVERTURE . . . . Accompanist
ACT ONE—
Scene:
Lab—   SUCH UNUSUAL WEATHER . . . . Junior, Lala
                    JUST A GOODY-TWO-SHOES. . . Grumby, Female Backups
                    DO I DARE TO DO IT? . . . . Junior, Lala
Bar—   TRY A LITTLE EVIL WITH ME. . . . . Junior
                    A SHARE OF PARADISE* . . . . Paradise, Junior
Lab—   METAMORPHOSIS . . . . Junior, Lala
Drugstore—   YOU'VE GOTTA GIVE HIM CREDIT. . . . Grumby, Junior,
                      Gretchen, Patrons
Lab—   I LOVE HIM . . . . Lala
Bar—   TRY A LITTLE EVIL WITH ME [reprise] . . . . Junior
                    IS IT SO WICKED TO WALTZ? . . . . Junior, Gretchen,
                    Patrons

ENTR'ACTE . . . . Accompanist

ACT TWO—
Scene:
Drugstore—   I LOVE HIM [reprise] . . . . Gretchen, Lala
                    THERE WON'T BE ANY WEDDING. . . Grumby, Gretchen,
                    Lala
Bar—   LIVE IT UP! . . . . Paradise, Lala, Gretchen
                    LONDONTOWN. . . . . Bartender, Patrons
Lab—   ONE MORE TIME . . . . Junior, Lala
                    ARIETTA PAZZA . . . . Lala, Junior, Grumby
                    FORMULA NUMBER THREE! . . . . All Survivors

*[If three acts are desired, end act with dance-exit by Junior and Paradise at climax of this musical number; then play "Entr'Acte" before raising curtain on Lab Scene which follows (and play it again, of course, prior to beginning Act Two [which will be your Act Three]) then continue show as written through Finale.]

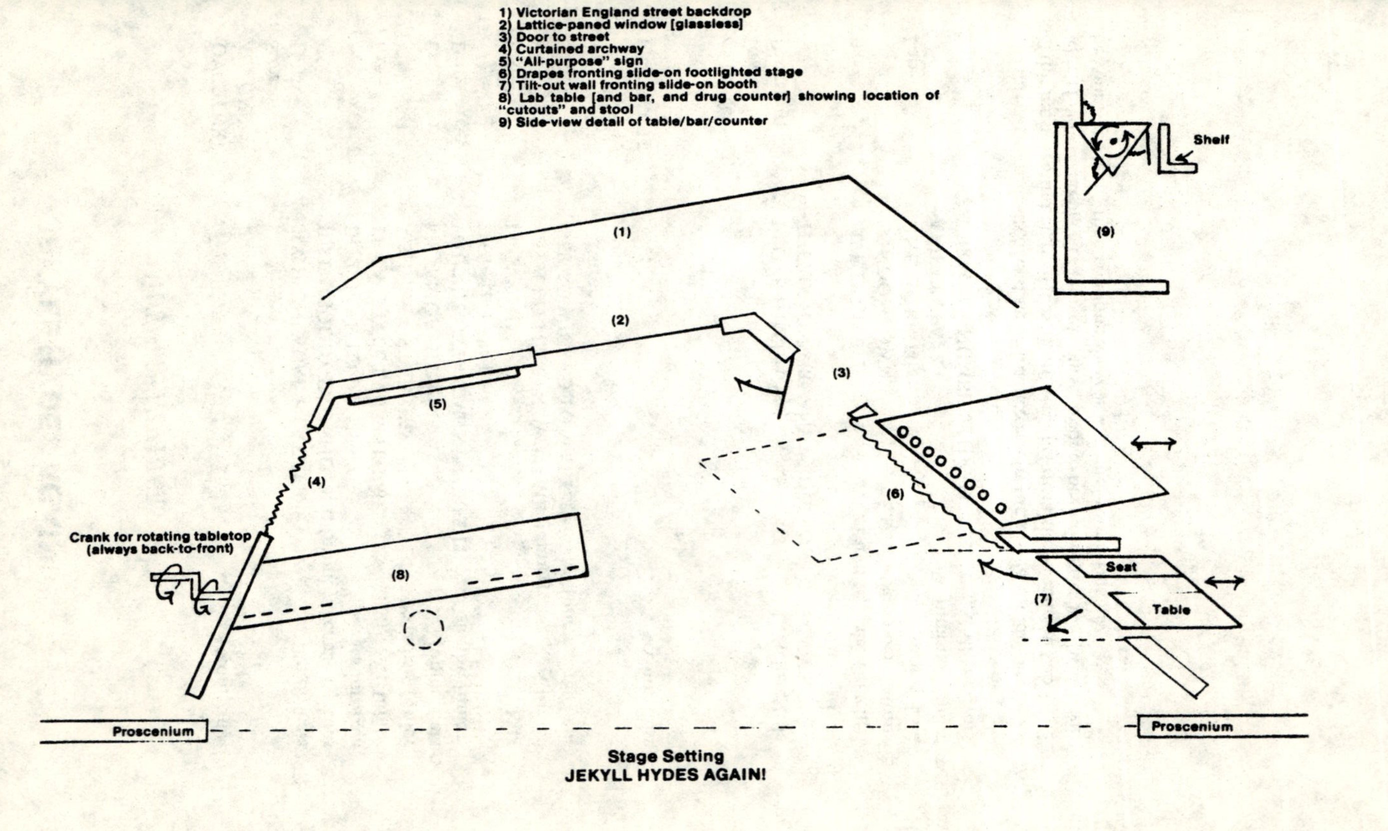

Stage Setting
JEKYLL HYDES AGAIN!

SPECIAL NOTE ON THE SET-STRUCTURE

Despite its three locales, this *is* a *one-set* musical (take a look at set-artwork, then come back here for explanation).

TABLETOP: This has three positions: Lab, Drugstore and Bar. To achieve each, table surface is rotated 120 degrees, and pop-up cardboard-or-plastic "typical props" (which are powered by a coil-spring on their upstage side) appear at the left and right *fourth* of the front of the horizontal surface (the central half, of course, is bare, so the performer upstage of the area can be seen clearly between them). These "props" are (and the more cartoon-style the artwork on these cutouts, the better for the ambience of the show) retorts, bunsen-burners, Florence flasks, etc., for the lab; aspirin, mouthwash, liniment, etc., for the drugstore; and various bottled liquors for the bar. If any *real* props are used (such as Jekyll's beaker-and-potion-flask), they should be on shelf (see set-artwork) out of view at upstage side of structure [CAUTION: *Never* allow a performer to set down *anything* on *top* of the tabletop, lest it go flying and smashing when top rotates!]. Surface of the tabletop must be at *least* four feet high — just below your Jekyll's chest-height — in order for stagehand to have room to creep beneath rotator-mechanism for various prop-placements (as in Jekyll's first change to Hyde).

ALL-PURPOSE SIGN: This wide, framed sign (about 5 feet wide by 3 feet high) bears the motto: "We Mix Stuff to Benefit Mankind". As you can see, the sign remains appropriate whether the scene is the lab, the drugstore *or* the bar. [NOTE: If you feel like being *really* ambitious, rig a rotator-mechanism to this sign similar to that of the tabletop, and use the same words with different styles of letters: Creepy for the lab, stark and plain for the drugstore, and colorful and cheery for the bar.]

STAGE/BOOTH: Both these items are *cheat*-angled for their maximum effectiveness re sightlines (see set-artwork), so that, for instance, patrons sitting on seat in booth will be visible to the audience when booth slides out into view. Front edge of stage-corners must be curved so as not to snag on drapes when stage slides into view (drapes will, of course, move aside via intrusion of stage-platform [which should be no more than 12 inches high, so

Paradise can step down to stage-level without breaking a leg]; for maximal effect, have a stage-*top* slide on above the stage-platform to widen gap in drapes even higher [drapes do *not* separate at the *top*; in this way, their parting will "frame" Paradise, and also allow them to close up again easily each time stage-platform is slid back out of view]). Two spring-hinged segments of wall which parts to admit booth (and forms upstage and downstage "backs" of booth), have this innocuous "saying" painted on them, thus:

**PLEASE ALLOW
US TO BROADEN
THE SCOPE OF
OUR SERVICE**

When it splits for bar-scene, of course, what the audience now sees on the (only visible) door is:

LOW
DEN
OF
VICE

TIMING: The shift from one locale to the next should take a *maximum* of five seconds, so the pacing of the show never lags.

JEKYLL HYDES AGAIN!

ACT ONE

Scene One

After overture, curtain rises on Lab. Lighting is dim. Through window, we can barely make out street in semi-darkness. There is continued sound of rain, gusty wind and thunder. Sporadically, lightning flashes outside, briefly illuminating street. During one such moment, we see JUNIOR JEKYLL crossing R-to-L outside window, hunched against the storm. A moment later, he enters through door; a small bell on a spiral spring over door tinkles on both opening and closing of door (this will happen, likewise, when this is the door to the Drugstore and the Bar). He rubs his hands together, blows on them to warm them, then goes behind lab table, bends from view a moment. Light flickers there, and he rises, with old-fashioned oil-wick hurricane-lamp in his hand (this is not a functional lamp; wick can be bearing a "flame" of red-and-yellow paper), and we see him clearly for the first time. He is pleasant of face, youthful of aspect, and his clothing is neat and clean, but not expensive in materials or cut. He "turns up" wick of lamp, and room brightens to about 3/4 full lighting. As he is setting lamp down on shelf (it will now be out of our sight, but room brightness will remain same), we catch a glimpse of LALA crossing R-to-L outside window, during another brief lightning-flash. A moment later, she enters through door, shuts it behind her. Then she sees JUNIOR and gives a little gasp.)

JUNIOR. *(Approaches her.)* I'm sorry if I frightened you, miss.
LALA. Yow *id* immy *naw*flskayr!

JUNIOR. I beg your pardon?

LALA. *(trying to enunciate more carefully)* Yow *id* immy nawfl-skayr!

JUNIOR. Do you know, young lady, if you would let me teach you proper English, in three months' time I could pass you off as a princess at the Embassy Ball!

LALA. *(Stares at him, makes a facial contortion, swallows very hard, and then says, quite clearly:)* Thank you, but there's really no need. I speak *quite* well enough.

JUNIOR. But — when you came in, you said, "Yow *id* immy *naw*flskayr!" You said it quite distinctly. Or do I mean indistinctly?

LALA. I was *trying* to say, "You *did* give me an *awful* scare!"

JUNIOR. Then why *didn't* you?

LALA. I had a piece of toffee in my mouth. Terribly chewy stuff.

(Storm-sounds cease, and all lights — inside lab and out on street — come up full.)

LALA. Oh! If that isn't the *strangest* thing! The storm seems to have ended. In which case, I'll just be going!

JUNIOR. Oh, *must* you?

LALA. Yes, I must. I only stepped in here to get out of the storm. *(Turns, opens door.)*

(Instantly, storm-sounds, etc., return at full peak; startled, she shuts door; and instantly, storm-sounds, etc., cut off; she pauses, and then — very tempted — she opens-and-shuts door as quickly as possible — and storm goes on-and-off just as quickly.)

JUNIOR. Excuse me, miss, but — *how* did you do that?

LALA. I *didn't!* I mean — it's never happened to me *before!* Probably just a coincidence ... *(Curious again, she opens door.)*

(Storm-sounds — she shuts it — storm stops.)

LALA. *(She shrugs and faces him again.)* A very *large* coincidence.

JUNIOR. Yes, it certainly *is.* Here — let *me* have a go at it ...! *(Does the door bit.)*

(Storm does the same.)

JUNIOR. Utterly and absolutely fascinating! *(Faces her.)* Do you know — it seems as though we — you and I — were somehow *meant* to be forced into each other's company!

LALA. Yes. Kind of *creepy,* isn't it!

JUNIOR. *(shrugs)* On a stormy day in London, what *isn't?! (Music intros, and he sings:)*

SUCH UNUSUAL WEATHER! WHAT A TREACHEROUS
    STORM!
GUESS WE'RE LUCKY TO BE INSIDE WHERE IT'S SO DRY
    AND WARM!
LALA.
SUCH UNUSUAL WEATHER! WHAT A PEEK-A-BOO SUN!
BUT WE'RE MAKIN' THE MOST OF IT WHILE SUNSHINE'S
    ON THE RUN!
JUNIOR.
WE CAN LOOK AT THE RAIN
POURIN' DOWN IN THE LANE—
BOTH.
WITH OUR SHELTERIN' ROOF OVERHEAD!
LALA.
SHOULD THE LIGHTNING NOT CEASE,
AND THE THUNDER INCREASE—
JUNIOR.
WE CAN ALWAYS HIDE UNDERNEATH THE BED!
SUCH UNUSUAL WEATHER!
LALA.
BUT I REALLY DON'T CARE!
JUNIOR.
HAD TODAY BEEN A LOVELY DAY,
YOU'D NOT BE HERE TO SHARE!
SO I'M BLESSIN' THE THUNDER AND RAIN FOR WHAT-
    EVER THEY DO!
BOTH.

THIS UNUSUAL WEATHER INTRODUCED ME TO YOU!

LALA.

SUCH UNUSUAL WEATHER! THOUGH I REALLY SHOULD
  GO,

EV'RY TIME THAT I TRY TO LEAVE, THE RAINDROPS TELL
  ME, "NO!"

BOTH.

BUT IF WE ARE TOGETHER, LET THE HURRICANE
  SQUALL!

WITH TWO ARMS THAT CAN HOLD ME TIGHT, I DON'T
  MIND IT AT ALL!

JUNIOR.

LET THE LIGHTNINGBOLTS FLASH!

LALA.

LET THE THUNDERBOLTS CRASH!

BOTH.

LET THE ROARIN' WINDS SHATTER THE SKY!

LALA.

THOUGH THE HEAVENS SHOULD BURST—

JUNIOR.

LET THE RAIN DO ITS WORST!

BOTH.

'CAUSE OUR HEATED EMOTIONS KEEP US DRY!

JUNIOR.

SUCH UNUSUAL WEATHER!

LALA.

WHAT A FURIOUS DAY!

JUNIOR.

THOUGH IT'S FOGGY, IT'S CRYSTAL-CLEAR

IT'S BROUGHT YOU HERE TO STAY!

BOTH.

GIVE A CHEER FOR THE THUNDER,

AND HURRAY FOR THE RAIN!

(By now, they are face-to-face in warm embrace.)

JUNIOR.

'CAUSE I CANNOT CONCEAL IT, NOT A JOT!

LALA.

I MUST REVEAL I CARE A LOT!

JUNIOR.
I'VE GOT A FEELING I DO NOT
REALLY HAVE TO EXPLAIN!
LALA.
DEAR, YOU NEEDN'T REFRAIN!
JUNIOR.
DARLING, ISN'T IT PLAIN!
LALA.
IN YOUR ARMS I'LL REMAIN!
BOTH. *(cheek-to-cheek, out front to us)*
BLESS THE THUNDER AND RAIN!
(On final accompaniment-chord, they keep cheek-to-cheek, roll eyes heavenward, smile inanely, and flutter their eyelashes, fast, in total ecstasy; then they unclinch.)

JUNIOR. Gosh, here we are, madly in love, and we don't even know our names!

LALA. *(uncertainly)* I know *mine.*

JUNIOR. Each *others'* names, I mean.

LALA. Oh. *(Nods in comprehension, then extends hand to him.)* My name is Lala.

JUNIOR. Your name is *what?*

LALA. Lala. Ell-ay-ell-ay; Lala.

JUNIOR. *(Takes her still-extended hand.)* A beautiful name. An enticing name. It's like the words in a lovely song when the singer has forgotten the lyrics. *(As she goes to reply, he continues, thoughtfully.)* Or Los Angeles twice. *(same business)* Or a bad misspelling of "Lili."

LALA. *(Turns her head away, coyly, very flattered.)* I like to think so. *(Then turns head back.)* But — what is *your* name?

JUNIOR. My name is Junior Jekyll, but all my friends call me "Junior."

LALA. *(Abruptly withdraws hand from his.)* With the name of Jekyll, it's a wonder you have any friends at all!

JUNIOR. *(Retrieves her hand, says with smarmy warmth:)* I have *now!* *(Both do cheek-to-cheek-eyelash-flitter, then back to normal, in unison; JUNIOR reacts to her hand's feel.)* Your little hand is so cold — if your name were Mimi, we could start crawling about in the hall to find your door-key!

Lala. *(wistfully)* I don't have a door-key. I have just recently arrived in London, and have not even a place wherein to live.

Junior. How dreadful! *(Clasps her upper arms, reacts, releases her.)* And you're soaked to the skin — drenched to the bone!

Lala. And sopping wet, besides.

Junior. *(Points toward archway behind lab table.)* Go into the other room and take your clothes off.

Lala. *(Recoils, hands clasped to her breast.)* How dare you!

Junior. *(Pats her on the head.)* It's all right, I'm a doctor.

Lala. *(instantly self-assured again)* Oh, good. *(Walks briskly through archway without looking back.)*

Junior. Such a lovely young lady!

(Door opens, and THADDEUS GRUMBY enters, flanked by the FEMALE SINGERS [henceforth known as "FS1" and "FS2"]; he stands inside door importantly and folds his arms, scowling at the young man.)

Junior. Good afternoon, sir. Is there something I can do for you?

Grumby. You can clear out of the neighborhood, sir!

Junior. I beg your pardon?

Grumby. My name is Thaddeus Grumby. I represent all the *right*-thinking people of this area. We want you to leave. Simple as that.

Junior. But — but *why?*

Grumby. Before you came here, this was a beautiful neighborhood, a sweet and gentle neighborhood, a charming neighborhood.

Junior. *(Gestures out window.) This?* This is a *slum!*

Grumby. *(triumphantly)* You *see?*

Junior. Now, just a darn minute—!

Grumby. How dare you address me in that tone! Has no one told you good manners dictate that one must always be polite to his *betters?*

Junior. Are *you* polite to *your* betters?

Grumby. I will be — if I ever meet any.

Junior. Look, I only came here today, fresh from medical school, to put my father's old place on the market, take the money, and start up my own practice. But you've made me just mad enough to stay!

GRUMBY. And follow in your demented father's footsteps, I have no doubt!

JUNIOR. You can't talk that way about my father!

GRUMBY. Oh, of course I can! After all, *he* was a crazed lunatic, going about the town causing all sorts of trouble — whereas *I*, of course, am nothing of the kind!

JUNIOR. Just who do you think you are, coming in here and telling a perfect stranger what he may or may not do?!

GRUMBY. Obviously, I think I'm the absolutely perfect man to do the job! *(Music intros, and he sings.)*
MAKIN' A DONATION TO A NEEDY CASE,
I WILL TOSS A COIN IN THEIR HAT,
UNLESS THEY'RE
OF THE WRONG RELIGION OR UNATTRACTIVE RACE,
AND THEN, OF COURSE, I LEAVE 'EM FLAT!
BECAUSE I'M
JUST A GOODY-TWO-SHOES, GOIN' ON MY WAY,
KEEPIN' ALL THE PEOPLE GOOD!
(JUNIOR reacts with startlement as the hithero-immobile and silent FS1 and FS2 leap into the song with GRUMBY.)
TRIO.
OH, YES, I'M/HE'S
JUST A GOODY-TWO-SHOES, WORKIN' NIGHT AND DAY,
CLEANIN' UP THE NEIGHBORHOOD!
(The ladies return to silent immobility for:)
GRUMBY.
WHEN I SEE A COUPLE SHARE A TENDER KISS
UNDERNEATH THE MOON IN THE LANE,
I ALWAYS
TIPTOE UP BEHIND 'EM AND INTERRUPT THEIR BLISS
BY WHACKIN' WITH MY BIG BLACK CANE!
BECAUSE I'M *[etc. through refrain with ladies; then:]*

WARNINGS FROM THE PULPIT NEVER CAUSE ME GRIEF;
HELL IS WHERE THE WICKED WILL FRY!
SO WHEN THE

PREACHER'S BREATHIN' FI—RE, IT'S A SWEET RELIEF
TO KNOW HE MEANS THE OTHER GUY!
BECAUSE I'M *[etc. through refrain with ladies; then:]*

UNIVERSAL GOOD IS MY UNWAVERING AIM!
   LADIES.
LOVE AND JOY AND PEACE HIS ONLY PLEA!
   GRUMBY.
AND SO, I'LL SPY AND PRY AND MEDDLE,
AND PUSH AND SHOVE AND MAIM,
(Ladies join him for:)
   TRIO.
TILL EV'RYONE'S AS SWEET AS ME!/HE!
BECAUSE I'M/HE'S JUST A GOODY-TWO-SHOES,
GOIN' ON MY/HIS WAY,
FROM MORNING TILL THE DAY IS DONE!
OH, YES,
(While ladies do backup-tra-la-la:)
   GRUMBY.
I'M JUST A GOODY-TWO-SHOES,
(Then they join him for:)
   TRIO.
WORKIN' NIGHT AND DAY
TO SCUTTLE EV'RYBODY'S FUN!
   GRUMBY.
GAMBLIN'S WRONG AND DRINKIN'S WRONG—
   LADIES.
AND SMILIN'S WRONG AND BLINKIN'S WRONG—
   GRUMBY.
AND LOVE IS WRONG, AND FUN IS WRONG—
   LADIES.
THE MOON IS WRONG, THE SUN IS WRONG—
   GRUMBY.
THE NIGHT IS WRONG—
   LADIES.
AND RIGHT IS WRONG—
   TRIO.
AND LET IT BE UNDERSTOOD

THAT I/HE CANNOT REFUSE USIN'
BOTH MY/HIS GOODY-TWO-SHOES,
CLEANIN' UP THE NEIGH ... BOR ... HOOD!
(Song over, he bows to ladies, they curtsey to him, then they exit to street and are gone; he closes door, then turns to face JUNIOR.)

JUNIOR. Do you always travel around with your own backup-singers?

GRUMBY. *(shrugs)* Doesn't *everybody?* *(Then, a return to his cold, businesslike manner.)* Now, Jekyll, you have had your warning: Go, go now, and all will be well. But if you persist on staying here—!

JUNIOR. Oh, pooh! You don't frighten me! Why, so long as I conduct myself in a dignified and moral manner, there's not a *thing* you can *do* to me!

GRUMBY. *(visibly frustrated)* I must admit — that is true enough. But one false step — one slip — one bit of ungentlemanly conduct, and—!

JUNIOR. Sir, I always behave as a proper gentleman should!

(LALA enters through archway, now wearing a flannel nightie.)

JUNIOR. *(Sees her and reacts, then says, a bit abashed, to GRUMBY:)* Well — *almost* always.

GRUMBY. Aha! A vicious *lovenest!* Now you *must* leave the neighborhood!

LALA. Lovenest?! Nonsense! Why, I simply had a headache, and came over to the doctor's for a remedy.

GRUMBY. Dressed like *that?*

LALA. What does it matter? After all, the man *is* a *doctor!*

GRUMBY. *(crushed by this telling blow)* Drat! I'd forgotten! *(Starts backing doorward, waggling forefinger at JUNIOR.)* But I warn you Jekyll — get out of line just *once*, and it's— *(Draws finger across own windpipe, making that "skrittzz" sound that conveys throat-cutting.)*

JUNIOR. Would you mind not spraying spittle on my floor? *(GRUMBY gives incoherent growl and exits, slamming door after him; JUNIOR turns to LALA in pent-up fury.)* Ooooh, what I'd like to do to that man!

LALA. Oh, here, darling, let *me!* *(Steps to door, opens it just as we see*

GRUMBY *crossing L-to-R outside window.)*

(Storm up full instantly; GRUMBY screams, covers his head, dashes from view; she shuts door, and storm stops instantly.)

LALA. *(She dusts hands lightly.)* There!

JUNIOR. *(Embraces her.)* That's a marvelous trick. You must teach it to me sometime.

LALA. *(unembracing)* But not now. You and I have a lot of work to do!

JUNIOR. We *do?* ... *We* do?

LALA. Look, Junior, *you* have a medical degree, and this is a laboratory, and you've decided *not* to sell the place in defiance of Thaddeus Grumby—

JUNIOR. How did you know *that?*

LALA. I eavesdrop.

JUNIOR. Oh.

LALA. *(picking up from where she was before his interruption)* —and as it so happens, *I* am a first-rate lab assistant—

JUNIOR. You are? Where have you worked?

LALA. Oh, here and there. I'm a *freelance* lab assistant. Going where I'm needed, doing what I must—

JUNIOR. Are you *sure* you're versed in the sort of thing I might be *doing?*

LALA. A lab assistant doesn't have to be. After all, my only function, should there be something you need which is out of reach, is to fetch it for you. If scientists had longer arms, there'd be no need for lab assistants at all.

JUNIOR. That's true enough. Oh, but — you a woman and I a man — what would people think?

LALA. Thanks to Thaddeus Grumby, they probably think the worst already, now that he's seen me in my flannel nightie.

JUNIOR. That reminds me — where did you *get* that nightie, anyhow?

LALA. I had it rolled up in my pocket.

JUNIOR. And it didn't get wet?

LALA. The rain was *out*side my clothing — the nightie was *in*side.

JUNIOR. Do you always travel around with a flannel nightie in your pocket?

LALA. *(shrugs)* Doesn't *everybody?!* *(then, brisk and businesslike again)* Now, then, shall we get to work?

JUNIOR. There is something I should tell you first.

LALA. And what is that?

JUNIOR. I shouldn't be able to *pay* you very much, I'm afraid. You see, I used up all my money at medical school. The only money I'd ever hoped to have was from the sale of this laboratory. If I don't sell it, I will be penniless.

LALA. *(Lays a hand gently upon his forearm.)* Junior, did I so much as *mention* money?

JUNIOR. *(brightens)* Why, no. You didn't!

LALA. *(Removes hand from his forearm.)* Well, I'm mentioning it now: No money and the deal's off! *(Starts for archway.)* I'd better get dressed and find me *another* lab to assist in. *(exits)*

JUNIOR. Drat.

LALA. *(off)* I beg your pardon?

JUNIOR. *(absently)* I accept your apology.

LALA. *(off)* Junior — are you absolutely sure your *father* didn't leave any money?

JUNIOR. *(Strolls upstage of tabletop, the better to converse.)* If he did, he never mentioned it. Of course, he didn't have much time for farewells, being gunned down so unexpectedly on this very spot. *(Thinks about that a second, then takes slight step to one side of the "very spot," visibly relaxes, and:)* You see, father had this formula — it was supposed to chemically separate the nature of man into either good or evil — shucking off the one and enhancing the other. Unhappily for father, he never *quite* got the *good* side into dominance. Every time he took the potion, he became a Mister *Hyde*, a creature of no morals whatsoever.

LALA. *(off)* What, none?

JUNIOR. Not a one. He thought nothing of drinking, womanizing, gambling, stealing—!

LALA. *(Pops out from other room, instantly, now re-dressed.)* Did you say *stealing?* Stealing things like — *money?*

JUNIOR. Why — I *suppose* so. I mean, after all, one doesn't go about stealing handkerchiefs or old newspapers.

LALA. Then I *have* it! Find this potion, become Mister Hyde, steal some money, and then you can afford my salary and we can live happily ever after!

JUNIOR. Oh, but honestly, Lala, I could never stoop to stealing.

LALA. Exactly my point. *You* couldn't — but Mister Hyde *could!*

JUNIOR. Never thought of that! ... Oh, but what's the use? I haven't the slightest notion where to find the potion.

LALA. *(Lifts bottle into view from shelf.)* What's *this* stuff?

JUNIOR. *(Takes it from her, reads label.)* It says "This is *it!* " ... Not very scientific labeling.

LALA. It's a small label — there probably wasn't room to write more. Take some.

JUNIOR. But dash it all — this might just as likely be furniture polish!

LALA. Hardly. This tabletop hasn't been polished since it was constructed!

JUNIOR. Good point. *(Uncaps bottle, raises it to lips, then lowers it.)* Shouldn't I have a *plan* first?

LALA. What *sort* of plan?

JUNIOR. Oh, little things like — where shall I *go* a-robbing, how shall I *accomplish* the theft without getting caught, what is my plan of *escape* if I *do* get caught — stuff like that.

LALA. Junior, you *can't* make a plan — that would make you an accessory-before-the-fact. Just take the nice potion and let *Hyde* figure out the rest.

JUNIOR. Oh, all right — but you'd better stand over there near the door.

LALA. *(Takes two steps in that direction, stops, turns.)* Whatever for?

JUNIOR. As I understand it, Hyde was *also* a fiendish *killer.* If it turns out he *still* is, being near the door would give you a chance to escape with your life.

LALA. *(nods)* Good thinking! *(Goes to door, turns, then frowns.)* Wait — I could lose valuable time turning the doorknob. I'd best have the door *open*, don't you think?

JUNIOR. It couldn't hurt. *(She opens door a crack.)*

(Storm comes up.)

LALA. *(She sighs and shuts door again, turns to face him.)* Yes it could. Oh, well, I'll take my chances. Have a sip of the potion, and I'll flee if necessary. Then you can go out, get some stolen money, come back here, change back to yourself—

JUNIOR. If I *can* change back. That was *Father's* problem, you know. He finally found he could become Hyde quite easily, but couldn't become himself at all, in the end. So when the *police* came by— *(Gives eloquent shrug, leaves tale unfinished.)*

LALA. That *is* a problem. Tell you what, then — take just a *teensy* sip. *That* ought to wear off soon enough.

JUNIOR. Yes, but possibly not *quite* before I've *murdered* you slightly. Still — scientific advance *is* for the good of mankind, so— *(Raises bottle to lips.)*

LALA. No, wait! I've had second thoughts. Perhaps I *could* be persuaded to work awhile for no salary ... it beats being knocked off.

JUNIOR. Oh, but being knocked off isn't an absolute *certainty,* Lala. The potion might just possibly unleash my *good* side, and you'd find yourself in here with the most marvelous man in the world.

LALA. *(brightens)* That *does* sound marvy! Do you *really* think it might *happen?*

JUNIOR. As a sane and sensible person, of course not — but as a scientist, I am not hampered by reason. *(Raises bottle to lips again.)*

LALA. Junior, wait! I've changed my mind. I'll work for you for free.

JUNIOR. I can't stop now, Lala. I must know how the potion works. After all, Father's discovery may prove an inestimable boon to mankind!

LALA. How?

JUNIOR. I haven't the *foggiest* idea. But scientists *always* talk like that.

LALA. That's true enough. Oh, but — aren't you the least little bit *afraid?*

JUNIOR. No. The truth of the matter is — I'm actually *hugely*

afraid! *(Music intros, and he sings:)*
DO I DARE TO DO IT?
THOUGH I TRY TO VIEW IT
AS A FORWARD STEP FOR GOOD,
PERHAPS I SHOULD
JUST LEAVE IT ON THE SHELF!
STILL, I HATE TO SCRAP IT;
IF THERE'S NO MISHAP, IT
COULD BE SUCH A BLESSING
TO FIND A WAY OF STRESSING
THE BETTER SIDE OF ONE'S INNER SELF!
I DON'T THINK IT'S SO WRONG ...
STILL, IF IT SHOULD GO WRONG,
AND I FOUND THE FORMULA DESTROYING MY BRAIN,
WOULDN'T I BE WISER
TO SIMPLY THROW
IT OUT? YET COULD
I SUR—
VIVE NEVER KNOW—
ING HOW MUCH GOOD
I
MIGHT EXEMPLIFY
IF I DIDN'T TRY
IT AND ASCERTAIN?!
(Once again raises bottle to lips.)
   LALA. *(Leaps to his side, takes bottle from his fingers, and sings.)*
JUNIOR, IF YOU ASK ME, THIS IS INSANITY!
OH, WON'T YOU THROW IT AWAY?!
YES, YOU COULD HELP MANKIND,
YET YOU COULD ALSO FIND
HYDE THERE TO GUIDE YOU ASTRAY!
OH, WON'T YOU LISTEN?!
I KNOW YOU MEAN TO BE NICE TO HUMANITY,
HOWEVER, IT COULD ALSO MEAN YOU'RE
PLAYING JEKYLL SENIOR'S GAME!
THINK OF THE DANGER
IF YOU BECOME
A HIDEOUS STRANGER!

GIVE IT UP, CHUM!
STAY NORMAL AND BURN THE FORMULA,
AND LEAVE MANKIND THE SAME!
(JUNIOR tries to take bottle back from her, she resists, and as they tug-of-war lovingly over the bottle, they repeat their individual melodies/lyrics in counterpoint; when song comes to its end, JUNIOR has possession of the bottle.)

JUNIOR. Stand back! My mind is made up! As a scientist I *must* find out how the formula works! *(Raises bottle, drinks deeply from it, sets it out of sight on shelf, then brings up other hand into view from behind tabletop and proceeds to take his pulse on the wrist of the hand which just put the formula-bottle away — and we see that the hand just now in view is a furry claw — although he doesn't; LALA reacts to it, of course, first visibly, then with an audible gasp, and—)*

[Let's hold it a minute, and explain a few physical facts about this metamorphosis into HYDE: When JUNIOR is fully *transformed, he will have two fur-covered hands with claw-like nails, and his head will have slightly longish hair with a very high forehead (the Benjamin-Franklin-look), and* one *double-width eyebrow, quite thick and furry, that hangs low and Neanderthalishly just above his eyes; he will* not, *however, have* fangs; *we* wanted *him to have fangs, but there is no way a performer can speak or sing with any clarity whatsoever with extra denture-work in his mouth, so we dropped the notion. Now that you know how he* looks *when fully transformed, let us explain how he* gets *that way: Let us assume your Jekyll is righthanded. Very well, then, he will tilt bottle with right hand, leaving his left hand dangling* far *from audience-view behind counter, so that an obliging stagehand underneath can slip a glove (backside of hand and backside of fingers thick with hair, and nails long and curving and sharp) onto unseen hand; this obliging person beneath the table will also glove the other hand, and finally place the "bald-wig with long top, side and back hair" upon Jekyll's head (that eyebrow is functional: It hides the line-of-demarcation between your Jekyll's real forehead/eyes area and the high-dome-bald area of the headpiece); got all that? Good. Now, back to the story: LALA gasps, and:]*

LALA. *Junior!* Your *hand! Look* at it!
JUNIOR. *(Holds furred hand at arm's length in direction of door,*

staring at it in fascinated horror — and *allowing* right *hand to dangle out of sight for that second glove* — *as he exclaims:*) My word! It — it looks — *different,* somehow ...! I — I wonder if it is an optical illusion? Perhaps it only *looks* horrible and furry ...?!

LALA. Why don't you *feel* it and *see?*

JUNIOR. Good idea! *(He does so, bringing up the* other *furry hand, of course, and we have same business: He does not notice the change.)*

LALA. *(Takes a few seconds for it to register, then she reacts, gasps, and:)* Junior! Your *other* hand! Look at *it!*

JUNIOR. *(Spins so that he now faces us from behind tabletop, splay-fingered hands before his face [palms toward him], staring at them in wonderment, during:)* Yipe! You're right! It's as furry as the other one! *(Then he gasps, eyes bulging, as hands start to strangle him.)*

LALA. Junior, what are you *doing?!*

JUNIOR. *(a strangled wheeze)* Nothing! It's the *hands! Hyde's* hands! I don't think they *like* me! *(Starts sinking slowly from our view behind counter.)*

LALA. Well, *stop* them! Fight them *off!* Get some kind of weapon!

JUNIOR. *(staring at her in chagrin just before vanishing)* What would I hold it with?! *(now is out of sight)*

LALA. *(Screams, dashes up behind left end of counter, on:)* Oh, this is terrible! Stop! *Stop!* Let *go* of yourself! *(Then she halts as HYDE — looking as already described — rises up into view, smiling evilly, chuckling horribly.)* Junior! Your *face! Look* at it!

JUNIOR. *(We will continue to* call *him "JUNIOR," even when he's HYDE, to avoid confusion for your JEKYLL-performer; his voice, as HYDE, will be a* bit *raspy and* slightly *lower in pitch, but not changed enough to garble anything he may say or sing; it's mostly evil-chuckly.)* I can see it reflected in your terrified eyes, my dear! *(Starts toward her, she backs doorward.)* What, afraid? Of old Mister Hyde? Why, *I* wouldn't hurt you, my dear ... *just* enough to make our romance — shall we say — interesting! *(Reaches for her with his furry claws.)*

LALA. *(back against door now) Wait!* Aren't you forgetting — the *money?!*

JUNIOR. *(Withdraws claws.)* The money! *Yes,* I nearly *did* forget! A man *needs* money to entertain a proper young lady ... *properly! (Shoves her aside, so that she falls to floor DL of door, yanks door open, exits on:)* I shall return within the hour! Do not *dare* to leave here! If I do not *find* you when I return — I will *surely* find you *later, wherever* you are — and you shall be *sorry* you ran away! *(Goes out, slams door after him; LALA groans, gets to her feet, runs sobbing to exit through archway.)*

END OF SCENE

ACT ONE

Scene Two

The bar. As stage and booth slide into view, BARTENDER rises (from squat) simultaneously into view behind bar as tabletop rotates bar-props into view; Lightning outside window goes dark at same time. MALE SINGER #1 (MS1) and FS1 are in booth as it comes into view, drinking. [Note: BARTENDER wears white shirt, bow tie, no jacket, sleeve garters, and a large handlebar mustache — when he doubles in POLICEMAN role later, he will be in uniform and no longer have the mustache, for a good visual contrast-of-characters.] As scene begins, BARTENDER is idly drying a glass with a towel, MS1 and FS1 are chatting in low voices, just loud enough so we can hear the sound, but not the words (after all, they are ad-libbing), as they chat. A moment after the scene begins, door opens and MS2 and FS2 enter together and go directly to bar in front of BARTENDER; their mood is jolly and their voices are light and cheery.

BARTENDER. Evenin', folks. What'll it be?
MS2. What's your pleasure, dearie?
FS2. Whisky. A double.
MS2. *(to BARTENDER)* And I'll have the same.

(As BARTENDER starts pouring their drinks, door opens and HYDE scurries in, chuckling; he goes directly to bar, and as BARTENDER sets whisky before FS2, HYDE picks it up and drinks it down.)

MS2. Here, now! Whatta you think you're doin'?! I ordered that for my lady friend!

JUNIOR. Then *you pay* for it!

MS2. *(Confronts HYDE.)* Listen, Mister, I don't like your attitude!

JUNIOR. *(Straightens, looks him right in the eye.)* And what do you intend to *do* about it?

MS2. *(abruptly uneasy)* Why, I — I ought to — uh —

FS2. *(Grabs his arm, tows him toward booth.)* It's all right. Never mind about him.

MS2. But I ought to—

FS2. Let it go, please, let it go. Somethin' *creepy* about that one — you can buy me another drink later. *(They will stand at booth, chatting quietly with FS1 and MS1, now-and-then glancing toward HYDE.)*

JUNIOR. That's the worst whisky I ever tasted! *(Grabs up other glass from bar, drains it.)* And so was that!

BARTENDER. Anything you say, sir, anything you say. Can I get you anything else?

JUNIOR. A *chair* would be nice!

BARTENDER. *(Instantly pulling bar stool into view, hands it to HYDE across bar; HYDE will place it on floor and sit, during:)* Yes, sir, comin' right up! Do you know — you look familiar — kind of like a feller used to come in here a lot — but o' course you can't be *him!*

JUNIOR. And why *not?*

BARTENDER. Why, *I* heard tell he was killed by the coppers. *You* seem alive enough.

JUNIOR. *(chuckles)* Don't believe everything you read in the papers! It's *me*, all right!

BARTENDER. *(startled)* Mister *Hyde?!* But I coulda *sworn* —?!

JUNIOR. Enough of your blathering! Get me something to drink — some of your *good* stuff, mind you! I've had a very hard day — snatching purses, picking pockets, mugging, assault and battery — takes it out of a man, let me tell you!

BARTENDER. *(Will be pouring drink from a different bottle.)* Then why do you *do* it — if I may be a bit nosy?

JUNIOR. Because it gives me great *pleasure*, of course! *(Music intros, and he sings.)*

LIVE YOUR LIFE AS THOUGH YOU MAY
NEVER SEE ANOTHER DAY!
JOIN IN MY PHILOSPHY:

TRY A LITTLE EVIL WITH ME!
EAT UNTIL YOUR BUTTONS POP,
DANCE AND DRINK UNTIL YOU DROP,
REVEL IN DEBAUCHERY—
TRY A LITTLE EVIL WITH ME!
EVEN THINGS THAT PEOPLE THINK ARE GOOD—
IF YOU DO THEM TO EXCESS—
YOU WILL BE SURPRISED HOW SOON THEY COULD
HELP YOU ON YOUR WAY TO WICKEDNESS!
SOME FOLKS' WEALTH IS MUCH TOO GREAT;
WHY NOT SHARE IN THEIR ESTATE?
STEALING MAKES FOR EQUITY;
TRY A LITTLE EVIL WITH ME!
HAVE A RED-HOT LOVE AFFAIR—
SEX WAS MEANT FOR US TO SHARE;
THAT'S WHY THERE'S ADULTERY;
TRY A LITTLE EVIL WITH ME!
EVIL TAKES SOME EFFORT, I MIGHT ADD,
YOU MUST BE COMMITTED TO IT.
IT'S NOT ALWAYS EASY BEING BAD;
THE WORK IS HARD BUT SOMEONE'S GOTTA DO IT!
BUT IT'S WORTH IT, YOU CAN BET!
LIFE IS SHORT, BE SURE YOU GET
YOUR SHARE OF INIQUITY;
TRY A LITTLE EVIL WITH ME!
TAKE A LITTLE EVIL ADVICE:
WHAT YOU WILL RECEIVE'LL FEEL NICE.
SO TRY A LITTLE EVIL,
TRY A LITTLE EVIL WITH ME!

(As accompaniment finishes, he raises now-filled glass in "toast" to BAR-TENDER, drains glass, clunks it down onto bar, chuckles.)

BARTENDER. Fill 'er *up* again, Mister Hyde, sir?

JUNIOR. Of course! *(while glass is being refilled)* You know, it's deadly dull in this place — what time does the floor show start?

BARTENDER. About half an hour from now, sir.

JUNIOR. Why wait till the last minute?! Start it now!

BARTENDER. Yes, sir, right away, sir, anything you say, sir! *(Steps to archway, calls through curtain:)* Hey in there, get a move on, we're startin' the show early!

PARADISE. *(off)* Oh, yeah?! And who says so?!

BARTENDER. It's a special request from our old friend, Mister Hyde!

PARADISE. *(off)* Luv-a-duck! Y're puttin' me on!

BARTENDER. Come out and see for yourself, then!

(A woman about 30, gaudily dressed, too much makeup, emerges through archway, steps to BARTENDER as if to speak, but he quietly points and gives a nod in HYDE's direction.)

PARADISE. *(She turns, sees him, reacts.)* Gorblimey! It *is* you! I thought you was bumped!

JUNIOR. Well, think again, my love! I've made a special trip here just to see you again! What do you think of *that?!*

PARADISE. Well, ordinarily, I hate surprises — but in your case, I'll make an exception! Buy a lady a drink? *(Will come around end of bar, move to him, during:)*

JUNIOR. Gladly — if I *meet* one!

PARADISE. Hold your nasty tongue, chum! Where do you get off, talking to me like that?! I'm *good* enough for the likes of *you!*

JUNIOR. *(shrugs)* Who *isn't?!* Bartender — a drink for our tawdry entertainer!

BARTENDER. The good stuff—?

JUNIOR. Of course not!

PARADISE. *(to BARTENDER)* Then *forget* it! Hard enough to sing and dance in this dump, without that rotgut of yours burnin' a hole in my belly! *(to HYDE)* And as for you, you cheapskate—! *(HYDE abruptly sways, fingertips going to temples.)* Say, now, chum, what's the matter? You look kinda funny ...

JUNIOR. *(voice almost returned to normal)* It's — it's nothing. I think maybe that the whisky is affecting me oddly — shouldn't mix chemicals indiscriminately, perhaps. I feel — it's horrible to admit — almost *human,* all at once!

PARADISE. Y' know, your voice almost *sounds* human, too! Maybe you're not such a bad bloke, *after* all!

JUNIOR. That's a *rotten* thing to say about me! I'm just as low and cunning and evil as I *ever* was! ... I hope.

Bartender. Beggin' your pardon, sir, but you owe me two-and-six for those drinks.

Junior. What—? Oh! Yes, of course, to be sure… *(Finds money in pocket, hands it over.)*

Paradise. Say, maybe you *are* off your chump, mate! First time I ever saw *you* pay for *anything!*

Junior. You don't know what you're talking about!

Paradise. I'm not so sure about that — it's funny, but — all at once — I get the feeling that somewhere down inside all that stinking rottenness is a genuinely *good* man, trying to get out!

Junior. That's the silliest thing I ever— *(Stops, fingers to head again, shuts eyes, moans.)* Oh …! I feel kind of— *(Opens eyes, drops hands, looks around.)* What — what *is* this place? *(Sees PARADISE.)* And — uh — whom do I have the honor of addressing?

Paradise. Why, it's *me*, Mister Hyde — Paradise Plotkin!

Junior. *What* name did you say?!

Paradise. Paradise Plotkin.

Junior. No-no, not *that* name — the other one! What did you just call me?

Paradise. Why — Mister *Hyde*, of course! It's your *name*, ain't it?

Junior. Uh — oh, sure, sure — yes, that's the name all right. Look — *(Slips down from bar stool, stands groggily.)* I think perhaps I'd better be getting home, before I change back completely — that is — I mean — See, it's *easy* to *grow* hair — *ungrowing* hair takes a little *longer* …!

Paradise. Change back? Change back to *what?*

Junior. It's — it's nothing. Really. But I'd better be going—

Paradise. *(Grabs his arm before he can pass.)* Not so fast, sport! I just got woke outa a sound sleep because *you* wanted the floor show *early!* You better not *move*, if you know what's good for you!

Junior. Floor show? What are you talking about?

Paradise. Just sit back up on that stool and *watch*, lover! *(Will stride to stage, step up onto it, turn and face into room, then call to BARTENDER:)* I'm ready when *you* are!

Bartender. Ladies and gentlemen—!

Quartet At Booth. *(They all look his way, speak in unison:)* Who — *us?!*

JUNIOR. *(getting back onto stool)* I wish you'd all stop shouting — I think I'm getting a headache!

BARTENDER. Don't worry, sir — *she'll* take your mind off it! *(to others)* May we humbly present — *Miss Paradise Plotkin!*

PARADISE. *(Music intros and she sings.)*
SAVE ALL YOUR SIGHS
FOR PARADISE!
WITHIN MY EYES
THE FLAMES OF LOVE RISE!
WHY TRY TO DISGUISE
YOU'RE CRAVING MY KISS!
YOU CAN'T IGNORE
YOU'RE ACHING FOR
THE CHANCE TO POUR
YOUR HEART OUT AND EXPLORE
THE START OF OUR BLISS!
(She will step sinuously down from stage and approach HYDE purposefully as she continues.)
SO MAKE A PASS!
DON'T BE A HIGHBROW!
IT'S SUCH A GAS
TO MEET A MAN WITH ONLY ONE EYEBROW!
WITH ME
UPON YOUR KNEE,
(Gets onto his lap.)
YOUR COURSE IS FREE AND CLEAR!
IT'S SO EASY, DEAR,
TO GO BREEZILY ON A SPREE!
(He puts his arms about her, tentatively.)
THAT'S THE SPIRIT, MISTER!
WHY FEAR THE GIST OF MY
IRRESISTIBLE SIGHS?!
(Slips from lap, starts circling him, fingers toying with the fringe of his hair, coyly.)
WHILE YOU I CARE FOR, PREPARE FOR
A SHARE OF PARADISE!
*(Music — which up till now has been a sultry habanera-tempo — will now shift to softshoe-with-break-tempo, and she and HYDE will dance to it; he

will not, however, start dancing until after he jumps from stool to stand beside her on floor.)

SAVE ALL YOUR SIGHS—

    JUNIOR.

WHY IS MY HEART SO LOUD AND FAST?

    PARADISE.

—FOR PARADISE!

    JUNIOR.

COULD I HAVE FOUND TRUE LOVE AT LAST?

    PARADISE. *[simultaneously with]*   JUNIOR.

WITHIN MY EYES	WHAT
THE FLAMES OF LOVE RISE!	A GHASTLY
WHY TRY TO DISGUISE	WAY
YOU'RE CRAVING MY KISS?	TO FEEL!

(He will now jump from stool, and dance with her as they continue:)

    PARADISE.

YOU CAN'T IGNORE—

    JUNIOR.

ALL OF MY NERVES ARE IN A KNOT!

    PARADISE.

—YOU'RE ACHING FOR—

    JUNIOR.

WHY IS MY COLLAR GETTING HOT?

    PARADISE.

A CHANCE TO POUR YOUR HEART

OUT AND EXPLORE THE START OF OUR BLISS!

    JUNIOR.

I CAN FEEL

MY BLOOD CONGEAL!

(Tempo abruptly becomes romantic beguine, and the two of them dance stageward in each other's arms, as they continue:)

    PARADISE.

SO MAKE A PASS!

    JUNIOR.

I'LL MISS MY BUS!

    PARADISE.

DON'T BE A HIGHBROW!

    JUNIOR.

WHY AM I COMBUSTING?

    PARADISE.

IT'S SUCH A GAS—

    JUNIOR.

WHAT'S TO DISCUSS—

    PARADISE.

—TO MEET A MAN WITH ONLY ONE EYEBROW!

    JUNIOR.

—WITH SOMEONE SO DISGUSTING?

    PARADISE.

WITH ME—

(Releases him as they start softshoe-tempo again.)

    JUNIOR.

WHAT AM I DANCING WITH HER FOR?

    PARADISE.

—UPON YOUR KNEE—

    JUNIOR.

WHY DON'T I KNOCK HER TO THE FLOOR?

    PARADISE.

YOUR COURSE IS FREE AND CLEAR!

IT'S SO EASY, DEAR,

TO GO BREEZILY ON A SPREE!

    JUNIOR.

I SHOULD SCRAM AND SLAM THE DOOR!

(But then, just as they get onto front of stage-platform, she bends him back in her embrace.)

    PARADISE.

THAT'S THE SPIRIT, MISTER!

WHY FEAR THE GIST OF MY IRRESISTIBLE SIGHS?!

    JUNIOR.

BUT SOMETHING INSIDE ME SAYS, "STAY

ANYWAY!"

(Music now becomes heavily-accented bouncy-march-tempo, and the two of them — doing high kicks that would do a Rockette proud — will start for exit at rear of platform through the flanking drapes there, on:)

    PARADISE.

WHILE YOU I CARE FOR—

    JUNIOR.

MY EVIL POTION—
  Paradise.
PREPARE FOR—
  Junior.
—LOVES THE NOTION—
  Paradise.
—A SHARE—
  Junior.
—OF EMOTIONAL DECAY ...!
  Paradise.
—OF PARADISE ...!
(And as they sustain final notes, they high-kick off stage platform through drapes, and others in bar applaud lustily.)

END OF SCENE

[and END OF ACT ONE, if you are doing show in three acts]

[Note: If you *are* doing the show in three acts, fine; you simply have the curtain fall. But if continuing *on*, be sure your players do *not* "drop out of character" by turning and walking off in full view of the audience as set switches to the Lab for the next scene: As soon as PARADISE and JUNIOR have *danced* off, BARTENDER should *stoop down* from view in a reverse-action to the way he first entered the scene (by the way, he should have removed the bar stool shortly after JUNIOR got off it to join the dance), and MS2 and FS2 should *step aboard* booth-platform containing MS1 and FS1, and ride off with it through the closing wall/doors. Smoothness of transition between scenes is vital to the pacing of the entire play.]

ACT ONE

Scene Three

The Lab. The next morning. Bright day outside window, and room interior is also bright. As scene begins, stage is empty, but a moment later, JUNIOR enters through door. He looks drained, haggard — but at least is no longer HYDE. He lurches in, shuts door weakly, then stumbles to left end of tabletop, grabs it, slumps against it.

JUNIOR. *(Calls hoarsely, wearily.)* Lala! *Lala!* *(Then he recoils, all energy now, as:)*

(LALA enters through archway on the run, her face furious, holding a large baseball bat [or cricket bat, if you want to remain regional] overhead, dashing right for him, on:)

LALA. *Murderer! Robber! Monster!* *(Then, just before bashing his head, recognizes him.)* Oh, it's only you. *(Lowers weapon.)*

JUNIOR. *(Half-crouched to floor, fingers laced atop skull, between table and door, slowly unlaces and rises, on:)* Ye gods, woman, whom were you *expecting?!*

LALA. Why, that dreadful Mister *Hyde*, of course! He made *ever* so many nasty innuendoes before he *left* here yesterday. What's *become* of him, anyway, come to think of it?

JUNIOR. The potion finally wore off. I would've been back sooner, but I've been walking the streets waiting for my hair to ungrow.

LALA. You poor darling.

JUNIOR. That's the last time *I* take that stuff! *Brrrr!* What a cold-blooded *creep* that Mister Hyde is! It was the weirdest feeling— I felt as though he were a totally separate person, and I was helpless, trapped inside him, watching his evil deeds and quite powerless to prevent him from doing them!

LALA. Just like your poor father, the poor man!

JUNIOR. My father? What are you talking about?

LALA. *(Starts back toward archway.)* I found his old *diary!* It's *not* the sort of thing a helpless young lady should read alone at night! *(Exits with weapon.)*

JUNIOR. *(Moves to area upstage of tabletop.)* You didn't look helpless waving that *bat* over my head!

LALA. *(Re-enters minus bat, plus large book.)* Never mind about that. Just *look* what your father wrote in this *diary!* *(Will lay book, open, on tabletop, so they can read from it, side-by-side, as music intros, and she sings:)*

"SOME VIALS OF CHEMICALS BROKE;
BUT THEN, IN A MASTERFUL STROKE,
WITH MORTAR AND PESTLE
I MIXED UP THE MESS TILL
IT STARTED TO BUBBLE AND SMOKE!"

JUNIOR. *(Also starts singing what he's reading.)*
"I LOOKED AT THE STUFF WITH A GRIN,
THEN FELT A STRANGE URGE FROM WITHIN.
I TOOK A SMALL DRAUGHT,
AND A LITTLE WHILE AFTER,
THE ROOM SLOWLY STARTED TO SPIN!"

BOTH.
"I FELT MYSELF TRANSFORM INTO SOMEBODY
WHOSE NATURE'S THAT OF HATE PERSONIFIED!
FOR PURPOSE OF MY SCIENTIFIC STUDY
I'LL CALL MY ALTER EGO MISTER HYDE!"

JUNIOR.
"AS JEKYLL I'M QUITE COMMONPLACE—"

LALA.
"AS HYDE IT'S A DIFFERENT CASE:"

BOTH.
"FUN-LOVING AND DASHING,
HIS HOBBY IS SMASHING

HIS FIST INTO SOMEBODY'S FACE!"

JUNIOR. (*Reacts to something on page, points at it while he sings to LALA:*)

OH, NO! OH, HOW UNBEARABLE!
THIS NEXT BIT'S REALLY TERRIBLE!
AS JEKYLL, HIS STAMINA STARTED TO CRACK!
HE CHANGED INTO HYDE AND HE COULDN'T CHANGE
  BACK!

LALA. (*looking where he points, and observing*)

SOME UNSUSPECTED PORTION OF
THE MIXTURE CAUSED DISTORTION OF
YOUR FATHER TO HYDE, AND ITS UNWITTING USE
CREATED EFFECTS HE COULD NOT REPRODUCE!

JUNIOR. (*with horror*)

MISTER HYDE SOON BECAME EPIDEMICAL—

LALA. (*wistfully*)

ALL BECAUSE OF SOME UNFORESEEN CHEMICAL!

BOTH. (*Again quoting as they read from book:*)

"BUT EVEN THOUGH I KNOW I MUST CONTINUE
TO TAKE THIS POTION, STILL I MUST CONFIDE:
WITH WICKEDNESS INFESTING EV'RY SINEW,
IT'S RATHER FUN BECOMING MISTER HYDE!
I KNOW THAT I WON'T BE CONTENT
UNTIL I DISCERN THE EXTENT
OF THIS MAN'S PERVERSIONS;
TO YET MORE EXCURSIONS
AS MISTER HYDE I MUST ASSENT!

(*Both straighten, but still read from book:*)

SO OBSERVE EV'RYTHING THAT I DO!
KEEP YOUR NERVE, NOW, HERE'S LOOKING AT YOU!
THIS EVENING I'LL BE OCCUPIED
AS MISTER HYDE!"

JUNIOR. (*Slams book shut as last chord of accompaniment sounds.*) Horrible! Horrible! Who would have dreamed it?! Some unsuspected impurity in his chemicals — some extra element he could not trace — and my poor father was unable to counteract his Hyde-side! (*Hands book to LALA.*) Here! Take this from my sight! I never want to look into its tragic pages again!

LALA. Of course, darling, of course! *(Will exit through archway with book, on:)* I understand your feelings completely.

JUNIOR. Did you notice the *date* of that final entry? It was the very day my father died! I wonder if he would have taken the potion that day had he known?

LALA. *(returning minus book)* I don't think he had a choice in the matter — from his notes, he seemed to have become a *monster-junky!*

JUNIOR. I cannot understand it — Dad was always so *careful* with chemicals!

LALA. Speaking of which — hadn't you better go out and *buy* some? We can't run a successful laboratory on nothing but lofty aspirations!

JUNIOR. But Lala — I don't have any *money!*

LALA. *What?* I thought you changed to Mister Hyde to *get* some!

JUNIOR. Yes, but if I remember correctly — I spent it all in a saloon.

LALA. Oh, Junior, how *could* you?!

JUNIOR. It was Hyde's idea, not mine!

LALA. Then there's only one thing to do — you must go to the drugstore and ask them if they'll let you have some chemicals on account!

JUNIOR. On account of what?

LALA. On account of you haven't any money!

JUNIOR. Oh, but, I can't simply go about asking for *credit!* I have no collateral to offer in exchange!

LALA. *(bustling him toward door)* Nonsense! I'm *sure* you'll think of *something*, Junior!

JUNIOR. Such *as?!*

LALA. Whatever it requires, whatever is asked of you, just *do* it!

JUNIOR. *(Opens door.)* All right, if you say so ... but are you really *sure?* I mean, I don't want to promise them simply *anything* in exchange for credit.

LALA. Believe me, whatever you have to promise, it'll beat the two of us sitting around *starving* to death!

JUNIOR. Good point. What will *you* be doing while I'm gone?

LALA. *(Starts toward archway.)* *I'm* going to delve a bit further into that *diary* — your father's Hyde-formula wasn't the *only* thing he invented, you know!

JUNIOR. It wasn't?

LALA. *(Pauses short of exit.)* Junior, the man was a dedicated *scientist!* He was inventing stuff for *years* before he came upon the transformation-formula! Unhappily for him, it was the *last* thing he ever concocted. But some of the *other* things might have a definite *commercial* value ...!

JUNIOR. *What?!* You would use my father's genius for merely making *money?*

LALA. Wouldn't *you?!*

JUNIOR. *(Hesitates; then:)* I asked you *first!*

LALA. Oh, get out of here and don't come back without lots and lots of lovely chemicals!

JUNIOR. You know, for an assistant, you're very bossy.

LALA. I plan to be your *wife* some day — I may as well get in a little *practice!* Now, scoot! *(She exits through archway, JUNIOR sighs and exits through door and shuts it after him.)*

END OF SCENE

ACT ONE

Scene Four

The Drugstore. Stage is empty. Then door opens and MS1, MS2 and FS1 enter, go to area downstage of right end of counter, start studying the products (those pop-up items) there, over the following dialogue:

FS1. It is most kind of you gentlemen to accompany me on my shopping excursion.

MS1. A young lady as lovely as you can never hope to gad about the town lacking male companionship.

MS2. But I *do* wish you would choose *between* us!

FS1. *(now standing before display)* But why should I? Then I would lose the opportunity to engender so much envy in the *other* young ladies of the neighborhood who do not even have *one* gentleman to escort them about the town.

(GRETCHEN GRUMBY emerges via archway; when she comes from behind counter, shortly, we will see that from her shoulders to the hem of her floor-length skirt, she is structured like an A-frame house; the young lady is pretty enough, in a pallid way, but obviously has a dire weight-distribution problem.)

GRETCHEN. Good morning, may I help you?

FS1. I was hoping to purchase a mustard-plaster for my mother. She has the lumbago something fierce.

GRETCHEN. I believe we have some in the storeroom. *(Starts from behind counter.)* If you will excuse me for a moment—? *(Exits through drapes, left [where the stage pops in during the Bar-scenes]).*

(Door opens and FS2 enters, strolls to area downstage of left end of counter, studies the displays there.)

FS1. *(noticing new entrant)* Why, Arabella! Walking out *alone* without a *gentleman*-friend?

FS2. *(Strolls right, to join trio before counter.)* When a young lady is as wealthy as I, she must be careful with whom she chooses to hobnob.

MS1 / MS2. *(Immediately turning backs on FS1, who pouts prettily as they eagerly face FS2.)* Wealthy, did you say? *(Quartet will now engage in quiet conversation, the visual import of which is that FS1 is trying to — and finally succeeding in her attempts to — get at least one of the young men re-interested in her; they do not do this pantomime broadly enough to distract from the main action of the scene, of course, which starts as:)*

(Door opens and JUNIOR enters; he is obviously in a nervous funk, and as he stations himself before the counter just downstage of the left prop-display, he is practicing his "approach" to the druggist aloud:)

JUNIOR. *(We can just hear what he murmurs softly.)* "Kind sir, you have a kindly face — I wonder if you would be kind enough to kindly—" That stinks. Let me see ... "Oh, merciful sir, I beg you, from the depths of my agonizing poverty—" Ha! For *that* one, I'd need a couple of backup-*violinists!* But there must be *some* way to—

FS1. Pardon, sir, but — did you speak to me?

JUNIOR. What—? Oh, no, I am most sorry, young lady. I was just — that is, I was trying to— No, never mind. Is the druggist in?

FS1. I have not yet seen him today, but—

GRUMBY. *(off)* Did somebody ask for the druggist—?! *(Enters through archway; sees JUNIOR, scowls.)* Jekyll!

JUNIOR. *(all hope lost)* Mister Grumby! Are — are *you* the druggist?!

GRUMBY. There is no shame in undertaking honest labor!

JUNIOR. Oh! Why — no, of course not. But — if it is *you* with whom I have to deal, I — I suppose I had just better turn and go.

GRUMBY. Nonsense! Whatever our personal differences, business is still business. I despised your father before you, but that did not prevent me from treating him like *any other* customer.

FS2. Excuse me, Mister Grumby—

GRUMBY. *(a terrifying roar)* Can't you see I'm *busy?!* *(She recoils.)*

JUNIOR. You treated Father like *that?*

GRUMBY. *(in once-again-polite tones)* Only when he wouldn't wait his turn. I cannot abide impatience in a person. Now, what do you want, I haven't got all day!

JUNIOR. I need a number of chemicals for my laboratory, I fear.

GRUMBY. But I *have* chemicals. What is there to fear?

JUNIOR. I fear I do not have any money with which to pay for them.

GRUMBY. *(Turns quietly to FS2.)* How may I be of *service* to you, young lady?

JUNIOR. *(Has started to turn away at this patent snub, but abruptly turns back before FS2 can reply.)* A moment, sir!

GRUMBY. *(Looks at him in narrow-eyed annoyance.)* Yesss—?!

JUNIOR. *Is* there no way I might establish a line of *credit,* perhaps?

GRUMBY. With what collateral?

JUNIOR. There is my laboratory—

GRUMBY. *(with a brief, impatient gesture toward archway)* I already have a laboratory, thank you.

JUNIOR. My medical-school *textbooks—?*

GRUMBY. I have no interest in reading.

JUNIOR. But surely there is *something—?*

GRUMBY. If there is, you have thus far failed to mention it.

JUNIOR. Oh, but sir — I would do anything — bargain anything — promise anything—!

GRUMBY. *(just as GRETCHEN enters through drapes with mustard plaster)* I am really most busy, Jekyll, so if there is nothing else— *(Espies GRETCHEN, turns suddenly shrewd.)* One moment — did you say ... *anything?*

JUNIOR. *(uneasy at his tone)* Uh — anything within *reason,* that is ...

GRUMBY. *(as GRETCHEN moves to quartet, turns over plaster to FS1, etc.)* Backing *down*, are you? I might have known a *Jekyll* would not be a man of his word!

JUNIOR. *(stung)* All right, then! *Anything! (then, less irate, more uneasy)* Uh — what exactly did you have in mind?

GRUMBY. *(Gestures toward GRETCHEN, who turns to face JUNIOR at the sound of her name.)* I would like you to meet my daughter, Gretchen.

JUNIOR. *(as if that alone were the bargain)* That's easy enough!... *(Bows politely.)* How do you do, Miss Grumby? *(Straightens, turns to GRUMBY.)* Now that I've carried out *my* end of the bargain—

GRUMBY. Jekyll, don't be such a *twit!* I have not yet *named* the bargain!

JUNIOR. Oh. I thought—? Well, then, just what *is* the bargain?

GRUMBY. If you truly desire a line of credit — at quite reasonable interest, I might add — all you need do is marry my daughter!

JUNIOR. But — I do not *love* her!

GRUMBY. *(Nods understandingly.)* And who could blame you! *(then, businesslike)* But that is exactly my point! *No* one could ever love a hopelessly plain girl such as she. I shall be encumbered with her until the day I die unless some gentleman takes her off my hands.

GRETCHEN. *(hurt)* Father! What a thing to say! And what a thing to bargain about! Why — I do not even know the young gentleman's name!

GRUMBY. His name is Junior Jekyll— *(with a hand-wave, making quick introductions)* Gretchen — Junior ... Junior — Gretchen. I hope you two will be very happy together — though I doubt that very much.

JUNIOR. But sir — to bargain with the fate of your own daughter—

GRUMBY. Do you want that line of credit, or do you not?!

JUNIOR. Why — yes — but — at such a price — still and all, though—

GRUMBY. *(rubbing his hands together in eagerness)* Yesss ...?

JUNIOR. Lala *did* tell me to do *anything* to get the chemicals I need...

GRETCHEN. Who, sir, is Lala?

JUNIOR. The woman I love above all others on the face of the earth.

GRETCHEN. What? You love another? Ant yet you would bargain for my *hand?*

GRUMBY. Don't be an idiot! He takes *all* of you, or the deal's off!

JUNIOR. Ah, me! Ah, me! But I do so desperately need those chemicals ... *(Squares his shoulders.)* Very well, sir — I accept your terms — *and* your unattractive daughter.

GRUMBY. Marvelous, marvelous! *(to quartet, who have been listening with interest)* Perhaps you did not *hear* me?!

QUARTET. *(in slight terror, echo him)* Marvelous, marvelous! *(Music intros, and they sing.)*

YOU'VE GOTTA GIVE HIM CREDIT FOR MARRYING HER!

GRUMBY.

ALTHOUGH SHE HAS TWO EYES, A NOSE, A MOUTH,
THE WAY THEY ARE ASSEMBLED,
YOU'D SWEAR HER FACE RESEMBLED
THE NORTH SIDE OF A DONKEY HEADED SOUTH!

QUARTET.

YOU'VE GOTTA GIVE HIM CREDIT FOR MARRYING HER!

JUNIOR.

SHE'S NOT EXACTLY WHAT I'D CALL PETITE!

GRUMBY.

NAME ANY FOOD, SHE'LL TRY IT;
THE ONLY TIME SHE'LL DIET
IS WHEN THERE ISN'T ANYTHING TO EAT!

QUARTET.

BUT THERE IS AN ADVANTAGE TO HIS DAUGHTER'S
    GIRTH!

GRUMBY.

THEY KNOW EXACTLY WHAT I'M THINKING OF!

JUNIOR. *(Nods, getting the point.)*

I'LL CERTAINLY BE GETTING ALL MY MONEY'S WORTH—

ALL BUT GRETCHEN.

BECAUSE THERE'S SO MUCH MORE OF HER TO LOVE!

JUNIOR.

YOU'VE GOTTA GIVE ME CREDIT FOR MARRYING HER:
A HAIRY GROWTH PERVADES HER LIP AND CHEEK!
 Grumby.
BUT TAKE IT FROM HER FATHER—
IT'S REALLY NOT MUCH BOTHER—
 Quartet.
SHE ONLY HAS TO SHAVE TWO TIMES A WEEK!
YOU'VE GOTTA GIVE HIM CREDIT FOR MARRYING HER!
 Grumby. *(to JUNIOR)*
YOU'LL NOTICE, WHEN YOU'RE FINALLY ALONE,
HER ODOR'S QUITE UNPLEASANT!
BUT AS A WEDDING PRESENT,
I'LL GIVE HER SEV'RAL BOTTLES OF COLOGNE!
 Quartet.
DON'T THINK THAT THIS EVALUATION'S CURSORY!
 Grumby.
SHE'S BEEN WITH ME FOR THIRTY YEARS THIS MAY.
HE'LL FEEL LIKE IT'S THEIR GOLDEN ANNIVERSARY—
 Grumby and Quartet.
JUST SEVEN WEEKS BEYOND THEIR WEDDING DAY!
 Grumby.
I'VE GOTTA GIVE HIM CREDIT FOR MARRYING HER,
ALTHOUGH IT'S ALWAYS CASH THAT I PREFER.
THIS TIME I WILL FOREGO IT,
BECAUSE AS YOU WELL KNOW, IT
WILL MEAN MY GRETCHEN'S WEDDING WILL OCCUR!
 Grumby and Quartet.
AS OFTEN AS WE'VE SAID IT—
 Junior.
THOUGH I WILL PROB'LY DREAD IT—
 Junior / All But Gretchen.
YOU'VE GOTTA GIVE ME/HIM CREDIT
FOR MAR ..... RYING HER!
(As singers sustain final note, and accompaniment plays out to its finish, JUNIOR follows a beckoning GRUMBY off through archway, a weeping GRETCHEN exits through drapes, and QUARTET exits out door.)

END OF SCENE

ACT ONE

Scene Five

The Lab. Still bright and cheery inside, but street outside window is somewhat darker, as in early evening. LALA emerges through archway, carrying small beaker of liquid; she is humming — with an occasional singing of a bit of the lyric — Such Unusual Weather as she busies herself with lifting the "This Is It" bottle from the shelf onto the tabletop, uncapping it, carefully pouring in contents of beaker, recapping bottle, and then shaking it to mix the ingredients; while she is in this last activity, JUNIOR — looking a bit guilty — enters through door toting two large bags labeled in large letters reading "Chemicals and Stuff"; during their dialogue, he will cross past her (upstage of her) and off through archway, then return immediately minus bags.

LALA. Oh, *there* you are! I was beginning to worry!

JUNIOR. No problem. Got all the chemicals we'll need for months! *(Exits with bags.)*

LALA. Now, *see?* I just *knew* you could do it, Junior. And just *wait* till you hear what I discovered in your father's notes — just the tiniest adaptation of the formula, and it will only take an *instant* to ungrow all that hair when the potion wears off!

JUNIOR. *(Re-emerging, joins her upstage of tabletop.)* That's nice.

LALA. Nice? Is that all you have to say, after all my delving in all those notes?! Your father's handwriting is nothing to brag about!

JUNIOR. Oh, yes, of *course* I appreciate all you've done. Very nice work, indeed. Lovely work. Fine. Just great.

LALA. Junior—? Is there anything ... *wrong?*

JUNIOR. Now, *what* makes you ask a silly thing like *that?*

LALA. *(Sets beaker and bottle out of sight on shelf.)* You — you don't seem *cheery* enough — I mean, considering *I* just solved that hair-ungrowth problem, and *you* solved the problem of getting the chemicals on credit—?!

JUNIOR. *(Clasps her fondly by her upper arms.)* Oh, Lala! Lala! Dear Lala! Sweet Lala! Darling Lala!

LALA. Oh, dear, now I'm *certain* something's wrong! What *is* it, dearest?

JUNIOR. *(Releases her, turns partly away.)* Well — it's like this — remember when you told me to promise *anything*, no matter *what* — in order to get those chemicals on credit—?

LALA. Why — yes, of *course* I do ...

JUNIOR. Did you mean it? I mean, *really* mean it? That I should promise *anything?* Anything at *all?*

LALA. *(very uneasy now)* Well ... yes ... I *did* mean it ... *then* ... but now, somehow ... I'm not so sure I *should* have ...

JUNIOR. Drat. That's what I was afraid of! I fear — I've gone too far!

LALA. Oh, Junior — you're frightening me! What sort of agreement *did* you make with the druggist—?

JUNIOR. Well — do you remember Mister Grumby—?

LALA. Oh! Who could *forget* him! That man — that odious man — horrible man! You should have nothing to *do* with *him,* Junior, *ever!*

JUNIOR. *(finally facing her again, wearily)* Well, for one thing — Mister Grumby is the druggist!

LALA. Oh, no! I do dearly dread to hear what bargain you have struck with that inhuman person!

JUNIOR. *(shrugs)* Okay.

LALA. But tell me anyway!

JUNIOR. *(trying to make light of it)* Well — it's the silliest thing — you'll probably laugh when I tell you — though perhaps not very heartily — but — you see — Grumby has a daughter, Gretchen — and she's no prize package, let me tell you — and Grumby knows it — and—

LALA. Junior, get to the *point!*

JUNIOR. All right. Gretchen and I will be married day after tomorrow.

LALA. *(recoils)* What? *What?* But Junior — *I* thought you were in love with *me!*

JUNIOR. I *am* in love with you!

LALA. But you're marrying *her?*

JUNIOR. Believe me, darling, I won't enjoy it for a minute!

LALA. *(with wry chagrin, out front)* Now, *there's* good news! *(then, to him, weepily)* Oh, Junior, how *could* you!

JUNIOR. Don't worry so, darling. Why, Gretchen is so grossly wide and heavy, she's bound to fall through the *floor* someday, and then you and I can be wed — after a suitable period of mourning.

LALA. But what if you live on the *ground floor?!*

JUNIOR. Drat. Never thought of that! *(Will take bottle from shelf, start uncapping it.)* Ah, well, it will all work itself out *somehow,* darling...

LALA. Junior — what are you *doing?* I thought you vowed never to take that potion *again?*

JUNIOR. That was before I met Gretchen! The woman positively turns my stomach! And yet — propriety demands that I take her out tonight to celebrate our engagement, and so — since *I* cannot face up to sharing her company — I thought perhaps *Mister Hyde* could! I mean, *nothing* is too revolting for *him* to enjoy...

LALA. But darling — won't she think it odd when a total *stranger* arrives to take her out?

JUNIOR. I've already allowed for that— *(Produces small flask from shelf, will start pouring a bit of the potion into it.)* I shall call upon her, take her out, and then — after she's had a bit of beer and gotten slightly smashed — I shall take the potion and no longer *have* to spend any time in her company — *Hyde* can round out her evening nicely. *(Will finish filling flask, recapping it and the bottle, and replacing bottle on shelf again, during:)*

LALA. Wait — surely the sort of evening *Hyde* would show her will displease *Mister Grumby* — *then* what will you do?

JUNIOR. Not to worry: Grumby, as a professional do-gooder, would never so much as set *foot* in the sort of establishments *Hyde* frequents. And what he doesn't know won't hurt me. *(Puts flask into pocket.)*

LALA. But if he should find out—?!

JUNIOR. I'll think of something. Well — must be toddling off. *(Goes to door, opens it, then turns for:)* When we are drinking our lovers' toast in champagne — I shall be thinking of *you!*

LALA. *(flatly, out front)* Yippee.

JUNIOR. I knew you'd be pleased. *(exits)*

LALA. *(Gives incoherent growl of rage, shouts doorward:)* Junior Jekyll, you are an absolute *birdbrain! (then, musing out loud)* Well, if he thinks I'd go on working for him *now,* happily dusting his bunsen burners while he's romping about with another woman, suffering in silence while he's nestling in her embrace, playing the humble lab assistant while he plays the devoted husband—! *(Slumps in weary resignation, says wistfully:)* He's absolutely right ... *(Sighs, music intros, and she sings.)*

WHAT CAN I DO?
WHAT CAN I SAY?
I URGENTLY APPEAL:
CAN ANY OF YOU
SHOW ME THE WAY
TO SHOW HIM HOW I FEEL?

I LOVE HIM,
BUT ONLY FROM AFAR.
LIKE SITTING ON A STAR,
HE'S SO FAR AWAY.

I'D TELL HIM,
BUT EV'RY TIME I TRY
MY THROAT BECOMES SO DRY
I CAN'T SAY WHAT I WANT TO SAY.

HOW CAN HE BE SO BLIND, SO UNAWARE?
HOW CAN HE FAIL TO SEE HOW MUCH I CARE?

I LOVE HIM;
BUT WHY CAN'T I REVEAL
THIS HUNGER THAT I FEEL?
WILL I EVER TELL HIM SO?

OR WILL HE EVEN WANT TO KNOW?

EACH SLEEPLESS NIGHT I'LL KNEEL ALONE TO PRAY
THAT IN THE MORNING HE'LL BE MINE TO STAY.

I LOVE HIM,
AND SOMEDAY, I INSIST,
HE'LL KNOW THAT I EXIST
AND MY LOVE FOR HIM IS TRUE,
ON THAT WONDERFUL DAY HE'LL LOVE ME, TOO!
(Starts to weep, exits through archway.)

END OF SCENE

[Note: We thought it nice to have a poignant and "straight" lyric for this point in the show; if you, however, would like just a *touch* of untoward humor in the song, for the 6th and 7th lines from the end of the song (beginning with "Each sleepless night..."), you may substitute in their place:

"I'LL SPEND MY DAYS IN WISTFUL YEARNING FOR
THE DAY THAT GRETCHEN CRASHES THROUGH THE
   FLOOR!"

But then please complete the final five lines as written; we have to draw the poignant line somewhere!]

ACT ONE

Scene Six

The Bar. Bright inside, dark outside window (but be sure the "spill" from lighting will illuminate any person who leans close to window outside to peer into bar). The set arrives similarly to its earlier appearance, with BARTENDER rising up into view as bar-top-"props" pop into sight, but this time, MS1 and FS1 are not in arriving booth, which is empty; a moment after scene-switch, PARADISE enters onto stage from L gap in stage-curtains, will move to L end of bar during dialogue with BARTENDER.

PARADISE. Crikey, what a slow night! If we don't get any customers in the next half-hour, *I'm* going to get out of these dancing-shoes and go to bed!

BARTENDER. I blame it all on that Mister Hyde — the way he acted, last time he was here — insulting the customers, drinking their drinks—!

PARADISE. Y'know, there was something *funny* about him, though — not quite as *mean* as I remembered him ...

BARTENDER. Couldn't prove it by *me!* Hope he stays away and *keeps* away — he fair gives me the *willies*, he does!

(Door opens and laughing group — MS1, MS1, FS1, FS2 — enters, heads for bar.)

PARADISE. Oops, I spoke too soon! Maybe things're livening up a bit!

BARTENDER. *(as quartet arrives before him downstage of bar)* Evening, folks — what'll it be?

FS1. Whisky!
MS1. Dry sack!
FS2. Gin!
MS2. Pint o' half-and-half!
BARTENDER. Comin' right up—! *(Then he reacts — and others also — and all chat and laughter cease, as:)*

(HYDE, accompanied by a rather nervous GRETCHEN, enters at door; the newcomers will make their way to a point midway between quartet and PARADISE downstage of bar; then:)

GRETCHEN. *(just a bit fuzzy of manner)* Junior — what *is* this dreadful place? Daddy would *surely* disapprove of you bringing me here!

JUNIOR. *(in chuckly HYDE-voice, of course)* What your Daddy doesn't know won't hurt him! And what *you* need is another drink or two!

GRETCHEN. But I'm so fuzzy-headed *already*, after that *last* place we stopped! Nothing *focuses* right — especially *you!*

JUNIOR. Perhaps you are merely seeing the *real* me, for the first time!

GRETCHEN. But I enjoyed our *last* stop *ever* so much more than *this* place! I mean, it had tablecloths, and waiters, and—

JUNIOR. Picky-picky-picky! You goody-goody people give me a pain! *(Music intros, and he sings [Note; He will start this song with HYDE-voice, but be about halfway-back to his JUNIOR-voice by its ironic ending].)*

FOLKS WITH MORALS MERELY WANT
WINE IN SOME RICH RESTAURANT!
ROTGUT'S NOT THEIR CUP OF TEA!
THEY DON'T FAVOR EVIL … LIKE ME!

WHILE THEY DINE ON CAVIAR,
I'M HERE IN THIS SLEAZY BAR,
WHERE GOOD FOOD YOU'LL NEVER SEE!
THEY DON'T FAVOR EVIL … LIKE ME!

THEY PRETEND THEY'D RATHER DINE IN STYLE,

BUT THEY ONLY DO IT TO ANNOY!
ANYONE CAN EAT WELL WITH A SMILE;
EVIL ISN'T EASY TO ENJOY!

FAWNING WAITERS AT THEIR SIDE—
FOOD THAT'S BROILED AND NEVER FRIED—
THEIR LIVES MOVE TOO EASILY!
THEY DON'T FAVOR EVIL ... LIKE ME!

NEVER SPLIT THEIR CLOTHING AT THE SEAMS;
NIGHTMARES NEVER WAKE THEM UP IN TERROR;
THEY GO OFF TO SLEEP AND PLEASANT DREAMS ...
I WONDER IF I'VE MADE A LITTLE ERROR?

THERE THEY GO IN SWEET DELIGHT—
HERE I WASTE A WEARY NIGHT—
AND THE REASON JUST MIGHT BE:
THEY DON'T FAVOR EVIL ... LIKE ME!

WHILE I'M LIVIN' LIFE LIKE A SWINE,
NICER FOLKS ARE FEELIN' JUST FINE!
THEIR LAUGHTER UP THEIR SLEEVE'LL
FAVOR LITTLE EVIL ... LIKE MINE!

PARADISE. Hey, now — you're beginning to sound almost *human*, Mister Hyde!

GRETCHEN. *What* did you call him?

JUNIOR. *(Quickly pulls her downstage, away from bar.)* Nothing! Nothing, my dear! You misunderstood!

GRETCHEN. But I could have *sworn* I heard her say—

JUNIOR. *Forget* about her! After all, your thoughts should be only for the man you shall *marry* two days hence!

GRETCHEN. Well — that's true enough, I suppose ... but *why* did she call you—?

JUNIOR. *(desperately) Enough!* That topic begins to bore me! Let us celebrate with a lovely waltz!

GRETCHEN. *(Recoils, horrified.)* A *waltz!* But — sir — *I* am a young lady of *virtue!*

JUNIOR. *(shrugs)* Who's *arguing?!*

GRETCHEN. But the *waltz* is *never* done by proper young ladies!

JUNIOR. Nonsense! Proper young ladies dance all the time!

GRETCHEN. Ah, but not *that* dance! They may perhaps do the minuet ... or, if feeling a bit more energetic, a pavane or a polonaise ...

JUNIOR. Then why not a *waltz?*

GRETCHEN. Isn't it obvious?

JUNIOR. If it *were*, would I be asking all these questions?!

GRETCHEN. Very well, then, I shall explain: In a minuet, a gentleman just *barely* touches the *fingers* of the young lady's hand ... in a pavane or polonaise, he might perhaps actually take hold of her *entire* hand ... ah, but in the wicked *waltz*, he actually puts his full *arm* about the young lady's — uh — about her — uh—

JUNIOR. *(with raging impatience)* Go on and *say* it! After all, I *am* a *doctor!*

GRETCHEN. Oh, that's right, I'd forgotten. Very well, then — he places his arm about her *waist* — and they press their bodies closely *together* — and, worst of all, when they *dance* thusly intertwined, they have been seen to actually *smile!*

JUNIOR. Oh, heavens-to-Betsy, girl! Is *that* all?!

GRETCHEN. Isn't that enough?! Any proper young lady would fear the ruination of her reputation in such terpsichorial combination!

JUNIOR. But she would *also* have the time of her life!

GRETCHEN. *Sir!* What are you *saying?!* (*Flees to booth, sits on R end of seat, hands clasped fearfully on the table-surface, avoiding his gaze.*) Oh, if my dear *Daddy* could hear you now, he would thrash you within an inch of your life!

JUNIOR. *(Approaches her, pleadingly.)* Aw, come *on*, Gretch! I tell you, it's a perfectly *lovely* dance!

GRETCHEN. That's not what *Daddy* says!

JUNIOR. Daddy-schmaddy! What does *he* know about having a good time?!

GRETCHEN. *(a bit swayed by this aspect)* Well — not *much*, I'll admit, but — I dare not indulge in such an unseemly pursuit!

JUNIOR. Don't be a dope! People are waltzing all the time, and are none the worse for it!

PARADISE. *(Since she and others at bar have been listening quite openly to JUNIOR and GRETCHEN.)* He's not *kidding* you, Miss ... a waltz is *ever* so much fun! *(to others)* Right?

OTHERS. *Right!*

JUNIOR. *(to bar group, annoyed)* Do you always eavesdrop on private conversations?!

OTHERS. *(shrug)* Doesn't *everybody?!*

JUNIOR. There, now, Gretchen — you *see?* Never mind what your Daddy says — use your *own* mind for a change — be *logical* — *think* about it! *Music intros, and he sings:)*

IS IT SO WICKED TO WALTZ?
WOULDN'T YOU WANT TO DANCE FACE-TO-FACE,
LOCKING A LOVER IN YOUR EMBRACE
AS IT STARTS!
HOW DIVINE!
IS IT SO WICKED TO WALTZ?
FEELING A BODY WITHIN YOUR GRIP,
SPLURGING THE URGE TO BE LIP-TO-LIP
WHILE TWO HEARTS
INTERTWINE!

GRETCHEN. *(Tempted, but still hesitant, sings uncertainly:)*
DADDY SAYS DANCING IS FROM THE DEVIL!
HAIR MAY GET MUSSED, AND YOUR CLOTHES DISHEVIL!

JUNIOR. *(gently taking her hand and drawing her to her feet)*
TAKE IT FROM ME, DARLING, ON THE LEVEL:
DADDY'S A DUD
AND A STICK-IN-THE-MUD!
(Draws her slowly—she's reluctant—to DC area.)
IS IT SO WICKED TO WALTZ?
WHO SAYS THAT HIDEOUS HARMS ABOUND,
WHEN THE GIRL YOU PUT YOUR ARMS AROUND
DOES THE SAME?
WHERE'S THE SHAME?

GRETCHEN. *(her resistance crumbling rapidly)*
BUT WHAT IF MY DADDY IS RIGHT,
AND IT'S BAD HOLDING TIGHT
AS THE MUSIC EXALTS?

JUNIOR.

IF DADDY SHOULD PICKET,
WE'LL TELL HIM TO "STICK IT!"—
(Draws her into his embrace on:)
 Both.
—AND WE SHALL BE WICKED AND WALTZ!
(All at bar — including BARTENDER — will move downstage into semi-circle about JUNIOR and GRETCHEN as the music soars gloriously and they dance for about seven beats, then "freeze" for spoken rhymed dialogue:)
 Junior.
If I gave you a dollar—?
 Gretchen. *(recklessly)*
I'd undo my collar!
(They waltz another seven beats, "freeze" again, and:)
 Junior.
For some new Paris dresses—?
 Gretchen.
I'd loosen my tresses!
(another seven-beat waltz, "freeze," and:)
 Junior.
If I bought you a house—?
 Gretchen. *(with mad abandon)*
I'd tear off my *bracelet!*
 Junior. *(His hopes dashed, observes dismally:)*
You're a *lousy* poet!
 Gretchen. *(Shrugs, observes matter-of-factly:)*
You're a lousy *date!*
(Then soaring waltz-music resumes, and others pair off — PARADISE with BARTENDER — and JUNIOR and GRETCHEN waltz, too, and:)
 Junior / Gretchen.
IS IT SO WICKED TO WALTZ?
 Others. *(overlap-echoing)*
IS IT SO WICKED TO WALTZ?
 Junior / Gretchen.
WOULDN'T YOU WANT TO DANCE FACE-TO-FACE,
LOCKING A LOVER IN YOUR EMBRACE—
 All.
—AS IT STARTS!
HOW DIVINE!

JUNIOR / GRETCHEN.
IS IT SO WICKED TO WALTZ?

   OTHERS. *(overlapping as before)*
IS IT SO WICKED TO WALTZ?

   JUNIOR / GRETCHEN.
LOCKING A BODY WITHIN YOUR GRIP,
SPLURGING THE URGE TO BE LIP-TO-LIP—

   ALL.
—WHILE TWO HEARTS—

   OTHERS.
—SLOWLY—

   ALL.
—INTERTWINE!

*(MEN and WOMEN, henceforth, will include JUNIOR and GRETCHEN
in their respective gender-group.)*

   MEN. *(continuing from last-sung word)*
—AND COMBINE, AND THEN—

   MEN / WOMEN.
MAYBE WE'LL LEARN THAT OUR LOVE WILL LAST, OR
MAYBE EMBRACING WILL BRING DISASTER,
BUT WHILE THE MUSIC IS SOARING FASTER,
ALL DADDY'S WARNINGS ARE PLAINLY IN VAIN!

   WOMEN.
IS IT SO WICKED TO WALTZ?

   MEN. *(overlap-singing)*
IS IT SO WICKED TO WALTZ?

   ALL.
WHO SAYS THAT HIDEOUS HARMS ABOUND,
WHEN THE GIRL YOU'VE GOT YOUR ARMS AROUND
DOES THE SAME?
WHO'S TO BLAME?

*(Music whirls/soars just a bit faster/louder as they dance blithely and wildly to
finish of song.)*
SORDID SENSATIONS WE MUST BEWARE,
AS THE AIR
STEAMS WITH DREAMS OF
DARK DISSIPATIONS, BUT WE DON'T CARE
WHILE WE'RE SHARING A FLAME

OF DESIRE!
WHY FIGHT IT?
THE FIRE
IS LIGHTED,
AND SHAME IS THE NAME
OF THE .... GAME!
(Sustaining final note, all waltz round-and-round the room as music rushes to its climax — and:)

(We see the horrified face of GRUMBY looking in through window from the street at GRETCHEN; he will remain there, over following dialogue, horrorstruck, till indicated differently.)

JUNIOR. *(As all halt on final chord, but each couple remains in full dance-embrace, during:)* Well, now, Gretchen! You have had your first waltz! What do you think of it?!

GRETCHEN. *(very primly)* It is low, vile, disgusting, sensual, degrading and reprehensible!

JUNIOR. *That's* true enough — but you still haven't answered my question: How did you *like* it?

GRETCHEN. I think I can safely sum up my answer in three words, sir—! *(then a veritable whoop of delight:)* One more time—! *(Music intros instantly, and GRUMBY pulls back from window and dashes for exterior of door, where he will enter, as all, dancing wildly, are already singing.)*

ALL.
IS IT SO WICKED TO WALTZ?
IS IT SO WICKED TO—?

GRUMBY. *(Now inside door, shouts in horror.)* Gretchen! *(Music cuts off; dancers stop — except for JUNIOR, who is flung by sudden halt onto his back on table of booth [hence out of our view for an instant] — and look toward GRUMBY.)*

GRETCHEN. *(terrified) Daddy! How* long have *you* been here?!

GRUMBY. Long enough to see my own daughter shattered and degraded in a public place! You're coming home with me this instant! *(Grabs her arm, starts towing her toward door, just as:)*

JUNIOR. *(Now abruptly converted back to himself, and no longer HYDE [via a quick change while out of view] — staggers into view again from booth, sees GRUMBY, and reacts in shocked embarrassment.) Mister Grumby!*

GRUMBY. *(at door, holding it open with one hand, other hand holding a weeping GRETCHEN's arm)* Aha! I might have *known* who would be scoundrel enough to be the cause of my daughter's degradation! *(very ominously indeed)* Jekyll ... I'm gonna have your *hide!* *(And as he exits with GRETCHEN, and JUNIOR slumps in misery, and PARADISE and others gather consolingly around JUNIOR, and an echo of waltz-music plays out to a rousing finish—)*

END OF SCENE

END OF ACT ONE

ACT TWO

Scene One

*The Drugstore. Full daylight, street in plain view. GRUMBY and
GRETCHEN behind counter; GRETCHEN is in tears, wiping at her
eyes with pretty kerchief.*

GRETCHEN. Oh, Daddy, Daddy—! How *can* you dash my hopes
this way?

GRUMBY. Better to be dead and buried, or to live life as a permanent old maid, than to be affianced to a man who would waltz you
in public!

GRETCHEN. But — I *love* him!

GRUMBY. Nonsense! Yesterday morning, you didn't even *know*
him!

GRETCHEN. But then I *met* him — and now I *know* him — and to
know him is to love him!

(Outside window, we see LALA moving L toward door.)

GRUMBY. My mind is made up!

GRETCHEN. Daddy, yesterday your mind was made up that we
would marry — if you could change your mind *then*, why not
change it *now?*

GRUMBY. *(Looks up as LALA enters.)* Enough of your blathering!
We have a customer! See to her needs! *(Starts to exit through archway
as LALA approaches downstage of counter, then turns, puzzled.)* Pardon,
Madam — but — have we met?

LALA. *(Wrestles with her conscience, temporizes.)* I am *certain* that no
one has ever *introduced* us, sir ...

GRUMBY. Mmmm, no, I cannot recall such an introduction. You must remind me of someone. I beg your pardon.

LALA. No offense. *(GRUMBY exits through archway.)*

GRETCHEN. How may I help you, Madam?

LALA. *(Lowers her voice conspiratorily.)* I am seeking the lady known as Gretchen Grumby.

GRETCHEN. Then seek no further, for I am she. And you are—?

LALA. I am known as ... Lala!

GRETCHEN. *(reacts)* "Lala"? Do you mean — the woman whom Junior Jekyll loves above all others on this earth?

LALA. *(sighs)* Ah, how I do wish that were true!

GRETCHEN. But it *is!* He told me so himself! And Junior Jekyll would not lie!

LALA. Naturally not. But perhaps he spoke the truth to you before that truth did alter with the intervention of successive circumstance!

GRETCHEN. What's that in English?

LALA. He *did* love me — until he met *you!*

GRETCHEN. What? Oh, do not torture my poor heart with false ambition! You are surely mistaken, Lala.

LALA. I have just come from his laboratory. He has not slept all night. He moans, sighs, continues to speak your name—!

GRETCHEN. And not yours?

LALA. Oh, yes, mine too ... but mostly to apologize for speaking yours.

GRETCHEN. Oh, dear. This is *joyous* tidings indeed— *(Ponders, tries again.)* These *are* joyous tidings indeed— *(Ponders, tries again.)* This is *indeed* a joyous *tiding—* *(Gives up, rephrases more succinctly.)* Lala, that's *neat-o news!*

LALA. I thought you would wish to know ... and now I must go.

GRETCHEN. Go? Go where? Back to ... *him?*

LALA. Fear not. My love for him is such that, even were I to work at his side forevermore, not an additional word of my innermost longings would he hear, since he prefers another.

GRETCHEN. You mean from now on it's hands off?

LALA. Would you not do the selfsame thing in my place?

GRETCHEN. Truly, I do not know. For, you see, my feelings for him are the sort that tend to overmaster a lady.

LALA. Alas, so are mine!

GRETCHEN. Whatever shall we *do?*

LALA. Whatever *can* we do? *(Music intros, and she sings.)*

I LOVE HIM—

GRETCHEN. *(overlap-singing)*

I LOVE HIM, TOO!

LALA.

—BUT ONLY FROM AFAR.

GRETCHEN.

WHAT CAN I DO?

LALA.

LIKE SITTING ON A STAR—

GRETCHEN.

HOW CAN I TELL HIM—

LALA. *(continuing in overlap with)*	GRETCHEN.
—HE'S SO VERY FAR AWAY.	—I CARE?
I'D TELL HIM,	WHY DON'T I KNOW
BUT EV'RY TIME I TRY	SOME WAY TO SHOW
MY THROAT BECOMES SO DRY	THE LOVE I'M LONGING
I CAN'T SAY WHAT I WANT TO SAY.	TO SHARE?
HOW CAN HE BE SO BLIND,	SHAMELESSLY TYING
SO UNAWARE?	MY HEART ON MY SLEEVE,
HOW CAN HE FAIL TO SEE	AIMLESSLY SIGHING,
HOW MUCH I CARE?	"IT'S JUST MAKE-BELIEVE!"
I LOVE HIM;	I WANT HIM SO!
BUT WHY CAN'T I REVEAL	HE'S GOT TO KNOW!
THIS HUNGER THAT I FEEL?	YET I STAY SILENT TILL
WILL I EVER TELL HIM SO?	MY HEARTBEATS ASK ME WHY
OR WILL HE EVEN WANT TO KNOW?	I'M AFRAID TO TRY!
EACH SLEEPLESS NIGHT I KNEEL	PASSIONS COMPEL ME
ALONE TO PRAY	IN VAIN, BECAUSE I'M
THAT IN THE MORNING HE'LL	FEARFUL HE'D TELL ME
BE MINE TO STAY.	I'M JUST WASTING MY TIME!
I LOVE HIM;	I MUST IMPART
AND SOMEDAY, I INSIST,	WHAT'S IN MY HEART!
HE'LL KNOW THAT I EXIST	BUT WHEN I TRY

AND MY LOVE FOR HIM IS TRUE;   I GROW SO WEAK
ON THAT WONDERFUL DAY   I CANNOT SPEAK, AND SO
HE'LL LOVE ME, TOO!   HE WILL NEVER KNOW!

GRETCHEN. Hey, hold on! I thought he *did* know you love him!

LALA. For that matter, *you're* not exactly keeping your feelings a secret!

GRETCHEN. Then *why* did you sing he was *unaware?*

LALA. Why did *you* sing that you stayed *silent?*

GRETCHEN. *(shrugs)* Oh — *you* know: Girls in love get goofy! *(laughs)*

LALA. *Don't* we, though?! *(Joins her laughter, then both stop instantly as:)*

(GRUMBY comes out through archway.)

GRUMBY. *(Points accusingly at LALA.)* Aha! I have finally remembered! *You* were the lady at Jekyll's laboratory in a *nightgown!*

LALA. *(annoyed, sniffs)* Never said I *wasn't ...!*

GRETCHEN. *(more and more distraught with each word)* What? Nightgown? Then ... you and he were — were — were—?!

LALA. *(impatiently)* Of *course* not! After all— *(partly to GRETCHEN, partly out front)* —this is a *family* musical!

GRETCHEN. *(instantly calm and cheery)* Oh, good.

GRUMBY. It is *not* good! It is vile and evil! And evil must be dealt with!

GRETCHEN. *(with apprehension)* Dealt with?

LALA. *(in trepidation)* In what way?

GRUMBY. In the two most painful ways possible: Romantically — and financially! *(Music intros, and he sings.)*
THE ENGAGEMENT'S OFF — HIS CREDIT'S DONE!

GRETCHEN. *(mourns aloud)*
NO MORE WALTZING — NO MORE FUN!

LALA. *(a bit introspectively, out front)*
I'M SAD FOR GRETCHEN — BUT HAPPY FOR ME;
WHAT IN THE WORLD SHOULD MY ATTITUDE BE?

(Note: In song that follows, GRUMBY and GRETCHEN, after he sings

his first solo part, will move about the room, he adamant, she following and begging and pleading, while LALA simply sings directly to us what's on her mind; by song's end, GRUMBY and GRETCHEN should be back behind counter, and LALA at door.)

GRUMBY. *(sings solo)*
THERE WON'T BE ANY WEDDING!
HIS BUSINESS WILL FAIL!
AND IF I CAN FIX IT,
HE'LL GO TO JAIL!
HE'LL GET, INSTEAD OF MY DAUGHTER,
BREAD AND WATER
TILL HIS HAIR TURNS GRAY!
THERE WON'T BE ANY WEDDING!
I'LL SURE SEE TO THAT!
WHAT JOY WHEN I TELL HIM
SHE'S DROPPING HIM FLAT!
HE'LL SOB, SIGH AND BELLOW,
BUT I'LL HAVE MY WAY:
THERE WON'T BE ANY WEDDING TODAY!
(Now GRUMBY starts moving about, GRETCHEN following.)
GRETCHEN.
OH, PLEASE, DADDY DEAR!
DON'T BE SO SEVERE!
I LOVE HIM SO!
AND HE LOVES ME!
CAN'T WE PLEASE FOREGO
THE STATUS QUO?
OH, PLEASE, DADDY DEAR!
DON'T WRECK HIS CAREER!
MY TEARDROPS STING AND SMART!
DON'T SEND TWO LOVERS SADLY APART,
OR YOU'LL BREAK MY HEART!
LALA.
OH, DEAR! WHAT SHALL I DO?
I'M FEELING QUITE TORN IN TWO!
CHEERY ... TEARY ... GLAD HE IS FREE ...
BUT SAD HIS CAREER IS UP A TREE!

I KNOW I'LL GET HIM BACK ...
ALTHOUGH HIS FUTURE IS BLACK!
SO, WHILE I AM WALKING ON AIR ...
I'M IN THE DEPTHS OF DESPAIR!
(Finally, GRUMBY sings his solo part again, and the ladies repeat their own solos in overlapping counterpoint with him, and all reach their Big Finish in those locales already cited, on:)

GRUMBY / GRETCHEN / LALA.
—TODAY! / —HEART! / —DESPAIR!
(As music finishes, GRUMBY exits through archway, and LALA opens door as if to exit, but:)

GRETCHEN. Wait! Do not go! We should share our sorrows together!

LALA. Do you mean weep upon one another's shoulders as properly-brought-up young ladies ought?

GRETCHEN. The *heck* with *that* noise! Let's go out and get smashed!

LALA. A marvelous ambition, indeed! ... Ah, but alas, I have no money whatsoever!

GRETCHEN. No more do *I!* ... *(Then, after a sly glance toward archway, suggests:)* But *Daddy* has a *cashbox* under the counter just *full* of the stuff!

LALA. Then what are we waiting for?!

GRETCHEN. *(Reaches below counter, comes up with twin fistfuls of bills.)* *I'm* ready when *you* are! Hold that *door! (She races from behind counter and out door, laughing wildly, and LALA — laughing just as wildly — follows her out, and closes the door with a slam behind her.)*

END OF SCENE

ACT TWO

Scene Two

The Bar. Dark night outside window. BARTENDER has risen into view behind bar as set changes. MS1 and MS2 arrive in out-popping booth. Door opens and LALA and GRETCHEN enter. GRETCHEN no longer clutches bills in her hands, and their mutual mood is glum. They move to position downstage of bar.

BARTENDER. Evenin', ladies. What's your pleasure?

GRETCHEN. Isn't that rather personal?

LALA. He means what do we want to *drink!*

GRETCHEN. Oh. Gosh, *I* don't know — we've had so many different drinks tonight *already ...*

MS1. Hey, look, chum! Unescorted ladies! *(Gets out of booth.)*

MS2. *(following him out)* If they're unescorted — maybe they're *not* ladies!

MS1. Well, there's only one way to find *out—!*

LALA. You know, what I *really* could use right now, is a cup of *coffee!*

GRETCHEN. I know what you *mean!* I couldn't even face French *champagne* right now!

MS1. Good evening!

GRETCHEN. Do we know you?

MS2. We'll be happy to introduce ourselves!

LALA. What do you want, anyhow?

MS1. Well, we saw you come into the bar, and we got right out of our booth—

MS2. —and came rushin' right over here to tell you—

GRETCHEN. *(before he can finish, to LALA)* Oh, wasn't that *nice* of them! I'm just *dying* for a place to sit down!

LALA. *(as she and GRETCHEN leave the flabbergasted men at the bar and head for the booth)* Thanks awfully, chums!

MS2. *(very glumly, to his companion)* Well, there's our answer—!

MS1. They're *ladies*, all right! *(Sighs, and falls into unheard conversation with his friend and the BARTENDER.)*

LALA. *(getting first into booth)* Do you know, I'd really rather be home in *bed* right now!

GRETCHEN. *(getting in after her)* Me, too — but fat chance of that! When my Daddy finds all that *money* missing, I won't get any sleep at *all*! More like three hours of sermons on theft!

(PARADISE has entered via rear of stage-platform on the line, headed for bar, but has stopped at the word "money," turned, sized up the ladies, and is now moving as-if-casually down toward booth.)

LALA. You could come home with *me* — I'm *sure* Junior wouldn't mind — we could put up an extra cot in the back room, and—

GRETCHEN. Lala, don't even *think* such a thing! If I'm due for a three-hour lecture for taking a little *cash*, can you imagine what I'll be in for if I spend the night with *Junior Jekyll?!*

PARADISE. *(Just arrived at boothside, reacts at name, gasps.)* Junior Jekyll? From where do you know—? *(Interrupts herself, recognizing GRETCHEN.)* Oh! You're the young lady was *in* here with him last night! *(Looks beyond her to LALA.)* But I don't seem to know *your* face ...?

LALA. You may call me Lala, Miss—?

PARADISE. Plotkin. Paradise Plotkin. And it isn't "Miss" — it's "Mrs."

GRETCHEN. And *I* am Gretchen Grumby, Mrs. Plotkin. Lately affianced to the Junior Jekyll of whom you overheard us speaking.

PARADISE. What? You're going to *marry* him?

LALA. *Was* going to marry him. But her father has forbidden it.

PARADISE. I see. And — where do *you* fit into the picture, Lala?

LALA. *(sighs)* I *love* him.

GRETCHEN. And *I* love him, too!

PARADISE. *(Nods understandingly.)* Alas — so do *I*!

LALA / GRETCHEN. *What?*

PARADISE. Oh, please do not think of me as a competitor, ladies — *my* love for him is a bit more on the *maternal* side — he *needs* mothering.

LALA. He needs a lot more than that!

GRETCHEN. He needs me for his wife—

LALA. He needs money for chemicals—

GRETCHEN. He needs a paid-up roof over his head—

LALA. He needs her father off his back—

PARADISE. See? It's just like I said — he needs *mothering!*

GRETCHEN. And marriage!

LALA. And an unhindered career!

PARADISE. I could just cry!

GRETCHEN. I could just sigh!

LALA. And so could I! *(sings)*

OH, WOE—!

GRETCHEN. *(joins her)*

OH, WOE—!

PARADISE. *(joins them)*

OH, NO!

(When they look up at her, she continues.)

THIS IS NOT THE WAY TO GO!

(Steps back a pace, sings.)

LIVE IT UP!

GET YOUR CHIN OFF THE FLOOR!

LIVE IT UP!

DON'T BE SAD ANY MORE.

WHAT GOOD WILL ALL THIS MELANCHOLY BRING?

YOU KNOW IT'S NEVER SOLVED A BLOODY THING!

LIVE IT UP!

DON'T JUST SIT THERE AND BROOD!

LIVE IT UP!

LALA.

WE'RE JUST NOT IN THE MOOD.

GRETCHEN.

MY ONLY HOPE FOR HAPPINESS IS GONE.

    LALA / GRETCHEN.

THERE ISN'T ANY REASON TO GO ON!

    PARADISE.

SO YOU LOST THE GUY;

THAT'S NO REASON WHY

YOU SHOULD SHOW SUCH EMOTION.

TAKE A TIP FROM ME:

THERE WILL ALWAYS BE

MORE FISH IN THE OCEAN!

PAINT THE TOWN!

YOU'VE GOT TROUBLES TO CHASE!

LOSE THAT FROWN,

PUT A SMILE IN ITS PLACE!

NOW'S THE TIME TO DINE

AND DANCE AND DRAIN THE CUP!

LIVE IT UP!

    LALA / GRETCHEN. *(as music continues)* But *we* both feel so rotten— ?!

    PARADISE. *(Shrugs their statement away, resumes singing.)*

LIFE IS ROUGH;

IT'S SOME FUN THAT YOU NEED!

(Will step back and beckon them out of booth, and they will get up, hesitantly, as she continues.)

THAT'S THE STUFF!

YOU JUST FOLLOW MY LEAD.

YOU'VE GOT SOMEONE WHO REALLY KNOWS THE
    SCORE.

I'VE DROWNED MY SORROWS MANY TIMES BEFORE!

    GRETCHEN. *(caught up into the spirit of the thing)*

HAVE A BALL!

    PARADISE.

NOW YOU'RE SEEING THE LIGHT!

    LALA. *(with growing enthusiasm)*

AFTER ALL,

WHO'S TO SAY SHE'S NOT RIGHT?

    GRETCHEN.

WHAT GOOD IS IT TO WALLOW IN DESPAIR?

PARADISE.
IT CERTAINLY WON'T GET YOU ANYWHERE!
   LALA. *(less cheery)*
BUT IT'S GETTING LATE.
   GRETCHEN. *(similarly)*
MAYBE WE SHOULD WAIT.
WE COULD DO IT TOMORROW.
(They start for door.)
   PARADISE. *(Follows them.)*
NO, THAT'S NOT THE WAY!
DON'T PUT OFF TODAY
WHAT YOU CAN DO TO SORROW!
(They turn to face her, almost at door, uncertain.)
THOUGH IT'S PLAIN
THAT YOU'VE TAKEN YOUR LUMPS,
WHY REMAIN
FEELING DOWN IN THE DUMPS?
DON'T BE SKITTISH!
   LALA. *(enthused again)*
GIVE YOUR TROUBLES THE SLIP!
   PARADISE.
BE VERY BRITISH!
   GRETCHEN. *(enthused again)*
WHERE'S THAT STIFF UPPER LIP?
(All three of them start for door.)

(Door opens as FS1 and FS2 enter — and the newcomers will look curiously at TRIO, but hold door open for them as they pass — almost dancing.)

   TRIO.
DON'T GIVE IT UP—
LIVE IT UP! LIVE IT UP!
(They dance out door on final sustained note, and newcomers let door close behind them, and head for the men downstage of the bar, on:)
   FS1. What was *that* all about?
   MS1. Don't ask!
   FS2. Wasn't that Paradise Plotkin with those ladies?

FS1. What's going to happen to your *show* tonight?

BARTENDER. Not to worry. Wasn't much of a show, anyhow.

MS2. But why would they *leave* a bar to go and live it up?

FS1. Is *that* where they're going?

FS2. Seems odd!

BARTENDER. Not when you consider all the bars and such there *are* in this city!

OTHERS. Well, *that's* true enough! *(Music intros, and all start to sing.)*

THERE ARE A LOT OF GOOD PLACES TO FROLIC
IN LONDON TOWN.
IT IS A MECCA IF YOU'RE ALCOHOLIC
IN LONDON TOWN!

(During song, group — including BARTENDER — will move downstage, and sing directly to us.)

YOU CAN HAVE FRANCE AND ITS WINE,
GERMANY'S BEER MAY BE FINE,
BUT IF YOU WANT A GOOD HANGOVER,
SAMPLE OUR GIN AND WHISKY!

MEN.
PEOPLE YOU PASS ON THE STREET ARE SO CHIPPER
IN LONDON TOWN.

WOMEN.
ALL EXCEPT THOSE WHO HAVE MET JACK THE RIPPER
IN LONDON TOWN!

MEN.
BOBBIES ARE THERE TO PROTECT—

WOMEN.
AND ONE THING YOU CAN EXPECT—

ALL.
THEY WILL BE WAITING TO TAKE YOU AWAY
IF YOU GET TOO FRISKY!

WOMEN.
VISITING ALL OF THE SIGHTS IS A THRILL,
YOU CAN BET.

MEN.
WHERE YOU'LL BE TESTING OUR PICKPOCKETS' SKILL,
DON'T FORGET!

Women.
STROLLING ALONG BY THE THAMES IS A TREAT HERE
IN LONDON TOWN
    Men.
DON'T MIND THE GARBAGE, THE RATS GOTTA EAT HERE
IN LONDON TOWN!
    FS1.
WHAT ABOUT LONDON BRIDGE?
    MS1.
I HEARD IT'S STILL FALLING DOWN—
    All.
IN LONDON TOWN!
    Women.
JOBS ARE A-PLENTY FOR FOLKS OF ALL AGES
IN LONDON TOWN.
    Men.
MOSTLY IN SWEATSHOPS FOR STARVATION WAGES
IN LONDON TOWN!
    All.
SHIPPING'S OUR NATIONAL PRIDE!
    MS2.
CAREFUL YOU DON'T GET SHANGHAIED!
    Others. *(to MS2)*
THAT'S NOT SO BAD, 'CAUSE A LONG OCEAN VOYAGE
IS SO RELAXING!
    Men.
COMMERCE AND INDUSTRY'S SECOND-TO-NONE HERE
IN LONDON TOWN!
    Women.
WATCHING THE BIGWIGS GET RICHER'S NO FUN HERE
IN LONDON TOWN!
    All.
EVEN THE WEALTHY COMPLAIN:
LIFESTYLES ARE HARD TO MAINTAIN
WHAT WITH THEIR PROFITS REDUCED 'CAUSE
THE PARLIAMENT'S ALWAYS TAXING!
THROUGHOUT THE EMPIRE, THE SUN NEVER SETS,
SO THEY SAY.

BUT WE CAN'T TELL 'CAUSE THE FOG ALWAYS GETS
IN THE WAY!
PEOPLE ARE BORN WITH A STRONG CONSTITUTION
IN LONDON TOWN.
WE REALLY NEED IT TO STAND THE POLLUTION
IN LONDON TOWN!
(They will stroll upstage — but move backward, so we can still hear them clearly — and BARTENDER will end up behind bar, and others at opened front door, as they move toward finish of song.)
THOUGH LIVING IN LONDON IS FUN
THERE IS ONE THING WE'LL SAY:
FOR LESS THAN A SHILLING
WE ALL WOULD BE WILLING
TO MOVE AWAY!
(All sustain final note as foursome exits, and door closes behind them, and BARTENDER starts to stoop down slowly from sight, because we are at:)

END OF SCENE

ACT TWO

Scene Three

The Lab. The following morning. Bright and cheery inside and outside window. Stage is empty, Then door opens and JUNIOR enters; he shuts door, and is just moving toward area upstage of tabletop when he reacts, looking down at [unseen by us] floor there, and stops, uncertainly. Then:

JUNIOR. Excuse me— *(No response. He tries a bit louder.)* Excuse me—?

(We hear a grunt, then a mumble, and then a feminine hand appears at upstage edge of counter, gripping it for support — then its companion-hand — and then PARADISE comes slowly up into view, sleepily scowling at the light.)

PARADISE. What *time* is it, anyway?
JUNIOR. Just half-past eight.
PARADISE. Then why's it so horribly *bright* in here?!
JUNIOR. It's a lovely sunny morning!
PARADISE. *(Stares at him a moment; then:)* Morning? You mean — there's an eight-thirty *ay-*em?!
JUNIOR. Paradise, what in the world are you *doing* there on my floor?
PARADISE. *(Shakes head, shuts eyes, puts fingertips to temples.) You* tell *me,* and then we'll *both* know!
JUNIOR. But surely—? *(He stops as:)*

(LALA, then GRETCHEN, emerge through archway, both looking about as frazzled as PARADISE.)

JUNIOR. Lala! Gretchen! What is going *on* here, a *pajama-party?!*

GRETCHEN. I never *wear* pajamas! ... Oh, but don't ever tell Daddy I *told* you!

LALA. Junior, we were all — well — living it *up* a bit last night — at least, I *hope* it was *last* night!

PARADISE. What *day* is it, Sonny?

JUNIOR. Alas, the very day that *was* to have been my *wedding* day!

GRETCHEN. Oh, good, then it *was* only last night we whooped it up!

LALA. But Gretchen — you haven't been *home* all night! What *will* your *father* say about it?!

GRETCHEN. *(sincerely)* Nothing that'll make me feel any worse than I do right now — I don't think I *could* feel worse than I do right now!

PARADISE. What *you* need is some coffee!

GRETCHEN. What *I* need is a new head! *(Starts back through archway.)*

LALA. The coffeepot's back on the left, on the rack over the bunsen burner!

GRETCHEN. *(off)* What's a bunsen burner? *(Then, as LALA opens her mouth to reply:)* Never mind — I found it!

JUNIOR. Ladies — just why *were* you out on the town? As I recall your circumstances — a broken engagement — a nearly-ended employment — a singer in a sleazy dive — you haven't much to celebrate.

PARADISE. But that's precisely the time a person *should* celebrate!

LALA. Right!

JUNIOR. Gee, what a great *song*-cue! *(Music: "False-Start Vamp"; then, as vamp ceases:)*

LALA. Too bad the authors didn't *write* one for this spot!

TRIO. *(shrug-sigh) Ah* well! *(Then, back to the plot:)*

LALA. Junior, whatever are we to do? Grumby will give you no more credit, and we will surely be out on the street if you have to close the laboratory!

JUNIOR. There's only one thing *to* do: I must become Mister

Hyde one more time, and get us all the money we need by committing the crime of the century!

PARADISE. No! No, don't do it! You *know* what it did to your poor *father!*

JUNIOR. Paradise — you *knew* my father?

PARADISE. Of *course* I did, Sonny — because — you see — *I* am your *mother!*

JUNIOR. What? That's impossible!

LALA. *Why* is it impossible?

JUNIOR. Because, for *one* thing, my mother's name was *not* Paradise Plotkin!

LALA. And for *another* thing?

JUNIOR. Paradise is obviously far too *young* to be my mother!

LALA. Perhaps she can explain both difficulties away?

JUNIOR. Hmm. Never thought of that. Let us ask her! Paradise—?

PARADISE. Easy as pie. For one thing, "Paradise Plotkin" is only a *stage*-name!

JUNIOR. I've been an imbecile! Why didn't I *think* of that!

LALA. And what is your *real* name?

PARADISE. "Paradise *Jekyll*"!

JUNIOR. You mean — for a stage-name — you altered your name to *"Plotkin"?*

LALA. It's certainly not something one associates with entertainment ...?!

PARADISE. *(shrugs)* You've seen my *act.* What *else* could I call myself?

JUNIOR. Good point.

LALA. Oh, but Paradise, what about the *other* thing?

JUNIOR. Yes! How can you possibily look too young to be my mother?

PARADISE. *Easier* than pie. You must remember, Sonny, your father's Hyde-formula was only one of *many* he concocted. That was his *first* formula. But his *second* was a mixture that, when drunk by a lady of any age whatsoever, would make her look thirty years old for the rest of her life!

LALA. Oh, how marvelous!

PARADISE. Not so marvelous as all that — I took the damn stuff before I remembered I looked like *hell* when I was thirty!

JUNIOR. Ah, but — why did you not tell me *sooner* that you were my mother?

PARADISE. What? You a young doctor, just out of medical school, to learn that your mother was a singer in a saloon?!

JUNIOR. It beats having no mother at *all!*

PARADISE. Hmm. Never thought of that. *(Flings out her arms.)* Sonny!

JUNIOR. *(Flings out his arms.)* Mammy! *(They embrace.)*

GRETCHEN. *(Peeks out from archway.)* How much coffee do I use per cup?

PARADISE. *(Disengages from JUNIOR, heads for archway.)* Oh, here, *I'll* do it! It's easier than explaining to you. *(Exits, and GRETCHEN exits again, too.)*

JUNIOR. Now, then, where's that Hyde-formula—? Ah, here it is! *(Lifts bottle into view from shelf.)* By the way, Lala, your additional chemistry worked just fine — the last time I was Hyde, the change-back was almost instantaneous — even ungrowing the *hair* took less than two seconds!

LALA. Even so — do not become that monstrous person again, I *beg* of you! What if you turned nasty and *murdered* me?

JUNIOR. We must not think of ourselves — we must think of science!

LALA. What's science ever done for *us?*

JUNIOR. That's beside the point.

LALA. Or for *anybody!*

JUNIOR. That, too.

LALA. Ah, but — with your engagement to Gretchen forever sundered by her dastardly Daddy — I had hoped that you — that I — that we —

JUNIOR. We can make our plans later. Right now, we need money! *(Raises bottle, starts uncapping it.)*

LALA. Can we not make our plans now? In that way — should you turn on me and render me dead — we shall at least have a happy *memory* — or *you* shall, at any rate!

JUNIOR. Oh, very well. After this last heist, let's get hitched!

LALA. *(Clasps her hands in joy.)* Such a beautiful plan!

JUNIOR. Glad you like it. And now— *(Raises uncapped bottle to lips.)*

LALA. Wait! Somehow, I am still fearful, I know not why!

JUNIOR. *(Exasperated, sets bottle down.)* Aw, Lala, for pete's sake, give me a break, will you?! *(Music intros, and he sings.)*
ONE MORE BRIEF LITTLE TEST,
THEN I'LL GIVE IT A REST!
ONE MORE TIME AS A BESTIAL FRIGHT,
THEN I'LL GIVE IT UP!
ONCE MORE DRINKIN' IT DOWN!
ONCE MORE PAINTIN' THE TOWN!
ONE MORE MERRY-GO-ROUND OF DELIGHT
TONIGHT!

LALA.
BUT I SEEM TO SENSE IT'S UNWISE!
WHERE'S THE FUTURE WE'VE PLANNED,
IF I DIE BY YOUR HAND?

JUNIOR.
WHY CAN'T YOU UNDERSTAND THAT
ONE MORE TIME COULDN'T HURT!

LALA.
BUT WHAT IF YOU CONVERT
ALL YOUR GOODNESS TO PERMANENT VICE?
IT ISN'T WORTH THE PRICE!

JUNIOR.
BUT DEAR, THERE IS NOTHING TO FEAR!
IT'LL BE A SUCCESS!
HAVE A HEART AND SAY "YES"!

LALA.
OH, WELL, I GUESS—

BOTH.
—THAT ONE MORE TIME
WON'T DO ANY HARM!
THERE'S NO CAUSE FOR ALARM!
ONE MORE ROMP IN THE SWAMP
AND THE SLIME ...
THEN WEDDING BELLS WILL CHIME
JUST ONE MORE TIME!
JUST ONE MORE TIME!

(At song's finish, JUNIOR raises bottle to lips — and:)

(GRETCHEN bolts out through archway.)

GRETCHEN. Stop! Don't drink! You've got the wrong formula!

(PARADISE also rushes out.)

PARADISE. Thank heaven we discovered it in time! *(Raises bottle into view.) This* is the Hyde-formula!

JUNIOR. I *don't* see why you're so *panicky!* What harm would there be if I remained thirty years *old* for the rest of my life?

PARADISE. Junior, you're talking about Formula Number *Two!* What *you* have there is Formula Number *Three!*

JUNIOR. And what does *that* one do?

PARADISE. We never found out — your father perished before he could test it on anyone — but I *do* know *this:* He told me that, if his theories were correct, it should be — could be — *only* taken by a woman, and when she took it—!

OTHERS. Yes? *Yes?*

PARADISE. It would permanently reduce her waistline six inches! *(GRETCHEN reacts instantly, and — others not seeing — takes bottle from where JUNOR just set it down, and sneaks off through archway, glancing back at them just once before departing, a smile of ecstatic anticipation on her face; OTHERS, of course, continue unawares.)*

JUNIOR. But Mammy — wouldn't that be a sort of *boon* to womankind?

LALA. Yes — think of it — no more diets — no more corsets—

PARADISE. Ah, but you forget the cardinal rule of chemistry and all the other sciences — *reciprocal reaction!*

JUNIOR. You mean — for every *positive* thing achieved — there is a countering *negative* thing achieved?

PARADISE. Yes! What the layman calls a "side-effect"! To get cold, one must give up heat—

LALA. To get light, one must lose darkness—

JUNIOR. Press one end of a lever down — the other end goes up! Yes-yes, I know, that's only basic scientific economics, what the textbooks in medical school used to call the Balance of Activated Matter.

Lala. But — Paradise — Mrs. Jekyll—

Paradise. Oh, start calling me "Mammy," Lala. May's well get used to it. What'd you want to know?

Lala. Well, Mammy — just what *is* the side-effect of Formula Number Three?

Paradise. That's just *it!* We never found out! So we daren't let it be used, until—

(Offstage, GRETCHEN screams.)

Trio. What was *that?!*

Gretchen. *(off)* Oh, no! No! Whatever am I going to *do?!*

Paradise. *(Rushes to archway, calls:)* Gretchen! What *is* it?

Gretchen. *(off)* Oh! Don't come in! *Please* don't come in!

Lala. *(now close behind PARADISE)* But Gretchen — we want to *help* you!

Junior. *(now close behind LALA)* Yes, dearest! What is the trouble?

Gretchen. *(off, miserably)* I drank some of Formula Number Three!

Trio. Oh, no! ... And what happened?

Paradise. I've *got* to look! *(Steps through archway; as JUNIOR and LALA attempt to follow, they are blocked by a re-emerging PARADISE who holds them off with her hands.)* No! Don't come in! You mustn't! Not yet! *Not* till I have — *done* something about the damage! ... Have you got a needle and thread?

Junior. Of course! *(Hands her small sewing kit from shelf; she exits.)* I wonder what she needs *that* for?!

Lala. *I* do not even dare to *imagine!* That poor, sweet Gretchen! I dread to think of what fate has so terrifyingly overtaken her!

Junior. Whatever it is — we will need *chemicals* to *undo* it! Lala — I no longer have any choice in the matter! *(Takes Hyde-formula, uncaps it, drinks, hands bottle to LALA, who will recap it and stash it on shelf.)* Soon — the crime of the century — and then — money-money-money-money!

Lala. Oh, my dearest — there is something you should know!

Junior. What is that?

LALA. I have been reading even farther in your father's diary, and have learned that the chemical addition I made, which speeds up the ungrowth of hair, *also* begins to limit the duration of the change!

JUNIOR. Lala — what are you saying?

LALA. That when you change to Hyde — you'll only *stay* Hyde for *five* minutes, *tops!*

JUNIOR. What? Lala! This is dreadful! *(Brings his hands up to clasp her shoulders — and his hands are the hairy Hyde-hands, now.)*

LALA. *(reacts)* Oh, no! Here you go again!

JUNIOR. *Aaarrrrgh! (Those hands are choking him again, of course; he will sink from view during:)* What shall I *do? I* can't commit the crime of the century in *five minutes!*

LALA. *(looking down to him [unseen now by us])* Well — then — how about the crime of the *week?*

JUNIOR. *(still unseen, but his voice a tinge* Hyde*ish)* In five minutes, I cannot even commit the crime of the *day! (Rises into view, reaching for LALA, Hyde-headed again.)* This is *your* fault! Cutting short my wickedness this way! I may only have five minutes — but that's long enough to make you pay! *(Then both react and turn as:)*

(GRUMBY enters through door.)

GRUMBY. *Aha!* I have you *now,* Jekyll! The police are on their way!

JUNIOR. *(Even in Hyde-guise, it's his own voice again.)* Police?! But — what for? Of what crime am I accused?

GRUMBY. For *one* thing, Jekyll, you have *abducted* my daughter!

JUNIOR. Ridiculous!

GRUMBY. I looked in her *bedroom* this morning, and her pajamas had *not* been *slept* in!

JUNIOR. She never *wears* pajamas! *(LALA covers her eyes, GRUMBY stares in triumphant loathing, and JUNIOR finally manages to say:)* ... Oops.

GRUMBY. Vile lecher! Despoiler of innocence!

(PARADISE pops in through archway.)

PARADISE. Have you got a scissors?

LALA. *(handing her pair from shelf)* What do you need *scissors* for?

PARADISE. Try not to *think* about it! *(Exits through archway.)*

GRUMBY. *(even more triumphant)* And consorting with a notorious *saloon*-singer!

JUNIOR. *(very definitely himself again, even if he still doesn't look it)* Sir, that woman you are speaking of happens to be my *mother!*

GRUMBY. *(wildly triumphant) Aha!* Not only a loathsome lecher — but the son of a saloon singer!

JUNIOR. Grumby — whatever your personal loathing for me, I still fail to see that I have done anything whatsoever to occasion your summoning the constabulary!

GRUMBY. Oh? How about committing *grand theft?!*

JUNIOR. *(uncertainly)* Is that an *accusation* or an *offer?*

GRUMBY. You know very well! Last night, my cash box was relieved of several hundred pounds!

LALA. That's not *so!* It was only *twenty* pounds!

GRUMBY. *Aha!*

LALA. ... Oops.

GRUMBY. Jekyll, you don't stand a chance — lechery, membership in a quite unacceptable family circle, and now — *theft!*

JUNIOR. Nonetheless, the law is no respecter of persons — my innocence of those charges shall be as a beacon leading the court to proclaim my acquittal!

GRUMBY. What's that in English?

LALA. He looks too nice to be a crook!

JUNIOR. *(Stares at his furry hands.)* Well — almost.

GRUMBY. Perhaps you do not know, then, that there has been a warrant out for the arrest of a certain *Mister Hyde* ever since the death of your late father?!

JUNIOR. Yipe! I *didn't* know!

LALA. Mister Grumby, If he *knew*, he certainly wouldn't have *changed* to Mister Hyde, *would* he?

GRUMBY. I refuse to banter about motivations! You are a lecher, your mother is a saloon singer, your assistant is a thief, and you are wanted by the police all over London! Jekyll, you are doomed!

LALA. *(Draws JUNIOR aside, says quickly, sotto voce:)* Junior! If you can change *back* before the police arrive, there is a chance you may survive!

JUNIOR. But Grumby grows impatient! If they do not arrive shortly, he may very well do me in, *himself!*

LALA. Then we must delay him from reaching that decision!

JUNIOR. How?

LALA. He likes nothing so much as the sound of his own voice! Let us provoke him to *use* it!

JUNIOR. Good thinking! ... But — *how* do we provoke him?

GRUMBY. What are you two blathering about? I grow impatient! If the police do not arrive shortly, I may very well do you in, *myself!*

JUNIOR. Horrors, Lala! I was *right!*

LALA. Fear not, my love! Just follow my lead! *(Music intros, and she sings to GRUMBY:)*

FIVE MORE MINUTES!
PLEASE HAVE MERCY FOR
FIVE MORE MINUTES!
NOT A MOMENT MORE!
IT IS SUCH A TEENY-TINY
DELAY THAT WE IMPLORE!

JUNIOR. *(Catches on, sings to GRUMBY, advancing on him at same time so that GRUMBY moves in general DL area, and JUNIOR and LALA can emerge from behind tabletop and get a bit more downstage for duration of song.)*

SCIENCE I'LL STOP FOR GOOD!
I'LL LEAVE THE NEIGHBORHOOD!
HENCEFORTH, I'LL SPEND MY LIFE
BEHAVING AS I SHOULD!

GRUMBY.
YOU MAY BE SINCERE,
BUT I MUST PERSEVERE!
STOP WASTING MY TIME WITH PLEADING!
MY DUTY IS QUITE CLEAR!

LALA.
HAVE MERCY!

JUNIOR.
TAKE PITY!

Grumby.

DON'T WASTE MY TIME!

Lala.

TAKE PITY!

Junior.

HAVE MERCY!

Grumby.

YOU FILTHY SLIME!

Junior / Lala.

RELENT, SOMEHOW! RELENT, SOMEHOW!

Grumby.

IT'S TOO LATE NOW! IT'S TOO LATE NOW!

Lala.

OH, WHERE IS YOUR COMPASSION?

Junior.

MY LIFE I COULD REFASHION!

Grumby.

YOUR CHIPS I'M GONNA CASH IN!

Junior / Lala.

PLEASE HAVE MERCY! HAVE A HEART!

Grumby.

NO MERCY HAS MY HEART!

(Then all sing simultaneously:)

Lala.	Junior.	Grumby.
FIVE MORE MINUTES!	SCIENCE I'LL	YOU MAY BE
PLEASE HAVE MERCY FOR	STOP FOR GOOD!	SINCERE,
FIVE MORE MINUTES!	I'LL LEAVE THE	BUT I MUST PER-
NOT A MOMENT MORE!	NEIGHBORHOOD!	SEVERE!
IT IS SUCH	HENCEFORTH, I'LL	STOP WASTING
A TEENY-TINY	SPEND MY LIFE	MY TIME WITH
DELAY THAT	BEHAVING	PLEADING! MY DUTY
WE IMPLORE!	AS I SHOULD!	IS QUITE CLEAR!

Lala.

HAVE MERCY!

Junior.

OH, PLEASE, SIR!

Grumby.

NO WAY!

LALA.
HAVE MERCY!

JUNIOR.
ON MY KNEES, SIR!

GRUMBY.
ENOUGH DELAY!

LALA.
FIVE MORE MINUTES! FIVE MORE MINUTES!

JUNIOR.
MERCY! MERCY!

GRUMBY.
I SHALL NOT BUDGE!
THIS IS YOUR JUDGMENT DAY!

LALA.
FIVE MORE MINUTES, PLEASE!
WON'T YOU DELAY—

JUNIOR.
PLEASE FORGIVE ME! LET ME LIVE,
AND I'LL ARRANGE TO CHANGE,
IF YOU WILL ONLY—

GRUMBY.
SO KNEEL AND PRAY!
MY MIND YOU SHALL NOT SWAY!

(And all finish simultaneously:)

LALA.	JUNIOR.	GRUMBY.
SIR, I PRAY!	LET ME GET AWAY!	NO WAY!

(At song's end, LALA is backed up against downstage center area of tabletop, GRUMBY is in DL area facing right, where JUNIOR has fallen to his knees, DC, on final phrase of song, hands clasped to his chest.)

GRUMBY. Enough! You must die! If the *police* cannot do it, why then, *I* shall!

JUNIOR. Ah, but could a *genuine* goody-two-shoes ever bring himself to *kill?*

GRUMBY. *(Blurts in his rage:)* I shall destroy *you* the *same way* I destroyed your *father!*

JUNIOR / LALA. *What?*

GRUMBY. ... Oops.

JUNIOR. What are you *saying?!*
LALA. *You* destroyed Doctor *Jekyll?!*
JUNIOR. My *father?!*

(PARADISE pops out through archway.)

PARADISE. My *husband?!*
GRETCHEN. *(off)* My late *father-in-law-to-be?!*
GRUMBY. Yes! I destroyed *all* of them! *(chuckling madly as he relives the moment)* It was *I* who gave him the impurities in those chemicals! I did it deliberately, *knowing* he would then be unable to change back into himself until he *died!* And he *took* it, and he *couldn't,* and he *did! ...* So there!
JUNIOR. *(Springs to his feet.)* Murdering monster!
PARADISE. *(stepping out just left of tabletop)* False friend!
LALA. Dubious druggist!
JUNIOR / PARADISE. *(looking at her in deep disappointment)* "*Du-*bious drug-gist"?!
LALA. *(hopefully)* "Fiendish pharmacist"?
JUNIOR / PARADISE. *Much* better! *(then, in quick rotation, to GRUMBY:)*
JUNIOR. Monster!
PARADISE. Traitor!
LALA. Fiend!
GRETCHEN. *(off)* Cowardy-cowardy-custard!
GRUMBY. *(annoyed, but intrigued)* Who *is* that back there?!

(GRETCHEN emerges through archway, standing proudly at center area upstage of tabletop.)

GRETCHEN. It is *I! (Others except PARADISE [who knows already, of course] react to GRETCHEN, first only with gape-jawed stares: Because she has quite obviously lost at least six inches from her waistline — and* gained *the same amount upon her* bustline, *as the now-fitted [thanks to PARADISE] gown very amply demonstrates; first to find his voice is:)*
GRUMBY. Gretchen! What — what has *happened* to you?!
GRETCHEN. *(no longer mousy, and very proud of her looks)* Face it, Father — your shrinking violet has blossomed — but good!

JUNIOR. *(Rushes to her, behind tabletop.)* Oh, Gretchen! You look so — your figure is so — the alteration is so—!

GRETCHEN. Ain't it the truth!

LALA. I don't understand?! Gretchen, if *that's* what Formula Number Three did to you — why were you *shrieking* about it?!

GRETCHEN. Because I blossomed so *fast*, I blossomed right out of my *dress!* I was afraid *Junior* might come running and *see* me thus exposed! *(Pronounces this "ex-PO-zed".)*

JUNIOR. *(to PARADISE)* So *that's* why you needed the needle and thread and scissors!

PARADISE. *(shrugs)* Why *else?* You see, Sonny, before this rotten rat betrayed my late husband and forced me into society's dregs, I used to be a pretty terrific dressmaker!

(At this moment, POLICEMAN enters shop, carrying gun.)

JUNIOR. Oh, no! *(Ducks from view behind tabletop [and, of course, will divest himself of Hyde-gear while out of sight.])*

PARADISE. Officer — I want you to *arrest* this man! *(Points at GRUMBY.)*

POLICEMAN. But — that is Mister Grumby, a respected druggist! *He* was the very man who *summoned* me, to deal with a certain Mister Hyde!

GRUMBY. Then stop your *babbling*, and *deal* with him!

POLICEMAN. You *don't* have to get *nasty* about it! Besides, where *is* he?

GRUMBY. *(Rushes upstage.)* Hiding from you, you numbskull, right behind this— *(Gets to left end of counter, looks behind it, gapes.)* He's *gone!*

JUNIOR. *(Enters through archway, behind GRETCHEN.)* Who is?

GRUMBY. Jekyll! Think you're pretty clever, don't you! Well, then, listen to *this! (Turns to POLICEMAN.)* Officer, this man last night abducted my daughter, robbed my cash box of hard-earned money, and is not only the son of a socially unacceptable saloon-singer, but of Doctor Jekyll, a man shot dead on these very premises but a few years ago! Whereas *I* — Thaddeus Grumby — am a neighborhood notable, scornful of the lower classes, impatient with evil, sworn to make this world a better place!

OTHERS. *And—?*

GRUMBY. Therefore, Officer, I command you to do your *duty*, as a *servant* of the *Queen!*

POLICEMAN. *(Touches his cap respectfully.) Right* you are, guv'nor! *(Raises gun, shoots; GRUMBY, a stunned look on his face, falls from view behind tabletop-area.)*

OTHERS. You *shot* him!

POLICEMAN. What *else* could I do? After all, I *am* a servant of the *Queen!*

OTHERS. *And—?*

POLICEMAN. *He* was a *royal pain! (Touches cap, exits through door, on:)* Have a good day!

PARADISE. Such a *nice* policeman! *(Moves downstage slightly.)*

LALA. *(moving downstage slightly)* Such a *pleasant* attitude!

JUNIOR. *(as he and GRETCHEN move from behind tabletop to downstage position between the other two)* Such a kindly *heart!*

GRETCHEN. *(with one final glance back toward [unseen] corpse)* And such a splendid *shot!*

PARADISE. Oh, Sonny, your troubles are all over!

JUNIOR. Well — not quite, Mammy.

OTHERS. Why *not?*

JUNIOR. Well, you see — I am madly in love with Gretchen — but on the other hand, I am insanely in love with Lala!

PARADISE. Well, then, Sonny — why not marry them *both?!*

GRETCHEN. *(delighted)* Could he *do* that?

LALA. Would the law *allow* it?

JUNIOR. Would the parson *perform* it?

PARADISE. Of course! Because Junior will have in his possession the *one* thing before which even the *highest* powers in the land must bow!

OTHERS. And *what* is *that—?*

PARADISE. *(Smiles adoringly at her son.) A note from his mother! (Others give loud cheer.)*

JUNIOR. *(Post-cheer, hugs LALA and GRETCHEN, one to each side, as he declares:)* Is there a happier man on the face of this earth — about to be wed to the *only women* he will ever love!

LALA / GRETCHEN. But darling — can you *support* two wives?!

JUNIOR. Of course I can! Because — we shall all be

incredibly *rich!*

OTHERS. We *will?! How?!*

JUNIOR. By going into the Beauty Business with Father's Final Formula! *(Music intros and he sings:)*
THINK OF OUR PROSPERITY
THANKS TO THIS DISCOVERY!
WAIT UNTIL THE LADIES SEE
FORMULA NUMBER THREE!
FATHER'S LAST EXPERIMENT
MAKES IT PRETTY EVIDENT
SALES WILL SOAR WHEN WE PRESENT
FORMULA NUMBER THREE!

LALA.
NOTHING MUCH REALLY CHANGES!

PARADISE.
ALL OF THEM'S THERE TO STAY!

GRETCHEN.
BUT IT JUST REARRANGES—

WOMEN.
—LADIES IN A LOVELIER WAY!

ALL.
WHAT WILL MOVE YOUR UGLY FAT
TO A BRANDNEW HABITAT?
WHAT WILL NEVER LEAVE YOU FLAT?
FORMULA NUMBER THREE!

PARADISE.
IF YOU WANT THE GUYS TO GAPE—

LALA.
BUT YOU'VE GOT A PUDGY SHAPE—

GRETCHEN.
WHAT WILL GET THEM GOING APE?

WOMEN.
FORMULA NUMBER THREE!

JUNIOR. *(in a falsetto, imitating "future customer")*
"WILL I BE FAIR AND FETCHIN'?"
(Back to normal voice, shakes head, smiling.)
BUYER'S WON'T HAVE TO ASK!
NOT WITH A SHOT OF GRETCHEN

FRONTIN' UP THE FRONT OF EACH FLASK!
    GRETCHEN. *(Reacts, gets uneasy.)*
WOULD YOU REALLY WANT ME TO
BE THUS IN THE PUBLIC VIEW?
THANKS, BUT NO THANKS! TOODLEOO,
FORMULA NUMBER THREE!
(Takes doorward step, but PARADISE intervenes.)
    PARADISE.
AS HIS WIFE, YOU CAN'T DENY,
YOU'LL BE IN THE PUBLIC EYE!
    LALA. *(Also goes to GRETCHEN.)*
WHAT'S WRONG GETTING GIRLS TO BUY
FORMULA NUMBER THREE?!
    JUNIOR. *(joining group)*
GRETCHEN, YOU'VE GOT TO TRUST ME!
WHY DO YOU LOOK ASKANCE?
BOOSTIN' THE BIGGER BUST, WE
GOTTA TAKE A MINIMAL CHANCE!
    GRETCHEN. *(Spoken, annoyed at his attitude:)* "We"?!
    JUNIOR. *(leading her downstage once more)*
HERE IS MY ANALYSIS:
I DON'T THINK THAT WE CAN MISS
ONCE WE START TO MARKET THIS
FORMULA NUMBER THREE!
    LALA. *(flanking them nearer GRETCHEN)*
THINK OF YOUR FINANCIAL CARES!
    PARADISE. *(flanking them nearer JUNIOR)*
WE COULD ALL BE MILLIONAIRES!
    JUNIOR. *(looking at GRETCHEN, but one hand thrust backward toward
archway at arm's length, pointing)*
POSING FOR THAT POTION *THERE'S*
YOUR RESPONSIBILITY!
    LALA / PARADISE.
HE'D LIKE TO POSE HIMSELF, BUT HE CAN'T!
    JUNIOR.
I'D HATE TO LOOK LIKE SOMEBODY'S AUNT!
    ALL BUT GRETCHEN.
LET YOURSELF GO AND POSE FOR

FORMULA NUMBER THREE!
Gretchen.
BUT THINK OF MY SHAME!
Junior. (*Inspired, face alight, clutches GRETCHEN by upper arms, singing triumphantly:*)
WE'LL LEAVE OFF YOUR *NAME!*
Gretchen. (*almost sold, but slightly uneasy*)
BUT WHAT IF FOLKS SAY IT'S *ME?*
Others. (*Extend hands pleadingly toward her.*)
WE NEVER WOULD SQUEAL!
Gretchen. (*Stands tall, sings out front:*)
ALL RIGHT! IT'S A DEAL
FOR—

[*Note: Hereinafter, "TRIO" means those not singing solo bit on the followup-
     lines.*]

Trio.
FORMULA—
Lala.
—FOR THAT LOOK SO HEALTHY!
Trio.
—FORMULA—
Paradise.
—THAT WILL MAKE US WEALTHY!
Trio.
—FORMULA—
Gretchen.
—THAT WE'RE RECOMMENDING!
Trio.
FORMULA—
Junior.
—FOR A HAPPY ENDING!
Gretchen.
FOR—
Junior.
FOR—
Lala.

FOR—
    PARADISE.
FOR—
    ALL.
FORMULA NUMBER THREE!
YES, THREE! YES, THREE!
YES, FORMULA NUMBER THREE!
(shouted:) Whee!
(And as foursome stands, downstage, holding hands [R-to-L: LALA, JUNIOR, GRETCHEN, PARADISE] and smiling with rapturous greed—)

THE CURTAIN FALLS

END OF SHOW

ALTERNATIVE FATE
FOR THADDEUS GRUMBY

There are those of you who may feel — with some justification — that our heinous villain "got off too easy" via that fast despatch by bullet. Never let it be said that Messrs. Sharkey and Reiser do not have a soft spot in their hearts for such; those of you who prefer a fate slightly more sadistic, twisted and devilish can substitute the following sequence where indicated.

[Pick up on GRETCHEN's post-shooting speech "And such a splendid shot!" *and continue thusly:]*

GRUMBY'S VOICE. *(At its sound, our quartet freezes in open-mouthed shock.) Fools! (Gives spine-chilling laugh.)* That bullet missed me by a mile! I merely fainted when he fired at me! And *now* shall I have my rotten revenge upon you all!

GRETCHEN. *(First to find her voice, as she and PARADISE turn upstage and move stage left a bit, while JUNIOR and LALA similarly turn and move stage right a bit, so that we have a clear view of the counter and upstage area.)* It's Father! He is yet *alive!*

JUNIOR. Then all our hopes are *dead!*

LALA. We can *always* send for that *constable* again!

PARADISE. Yes! Why *don't* we?!

GRUMBY'S VOICE. Because your time has run out! The moment I came to, I determined to rid the earth of you singlehanded! To this end, Jekyll, I have filched the flask of your father's foul formula, drunk deeply of it, and now shall I — in the guise of the monstrous Mister Hyde — commit carnage upon you all!

QUARTET. *(cringing in unison) Oh, nooooo!*

(And then GRUMBY rises from behind counter, face contorted with

malevolence — and his bosom protruding with bulges as large as a pair of volleyballs; QUARTET reacts, fear turns to hilarity, and they howl with laughter, almost sobbing on one another's shoulders in unholy glee.)

GRUMBY. What's so funny?! *(Then looks down at himself.)* Oh, no! I took the wrong flask! This is ghastly! Quickly — where is the antidote?!

QUARTET. There *isn't* any!

GRUMBY. *(stumbling doorward in hysterical panic)* This is a nightmare! I shall nevermore be able to show my face in this city again!

JUNIOR. Believe me, Grumby, if you go out in public like *that,* your *face* is the *last* thing anybody will be looking at! *(With a shrill cry of despair, GRUMBY bolts through door, rushes L-to-R outside window, and is gone forever.)*

[Now pick up with PARADISE's "Oh, Sonny, your troubles are all over!" and continue to end of play as written.]

ADDITIONAL PRODUCTION NOTES

There is probably a host of different ways of staging "JEKYLL HYDES AGAIN!", and we would like to go on record as saying — if you have a different method — go to it, and more power to you. Though we both finally settled on the stage setting as pictured in the artwork, we had other options we simply didn't exercise (or this would be a bookful of stage-settings with no room for the show itself!); some of them might be of interest to you, however, in considering how to go about doing the show:

1) THE ALL-PURPOSE SIGN: We put it on the wall of the flat behind the tabletop/counter/bar; it can also just as well be the *front* of the tabletop/counter/bar *itself*, and then you can make the upstage left window twice as wide, filling the entire flat upstage of the action of the show.

2) THE STAGE-FLANKING DRAPES: If the mechanics of this pose a problem for you, you might instead want the entire wall in front of that on-again-off-again stage platform to swing *up*, on hinges, thus forming a *ceiling* for the stage whenever it emerges; if you *do* go this route, however, remember that you still need some sort of exit in that wall for GRETCHEN to go to the storeroom in the first drugstore-scene.

3) THE ROTATING TABLETOP: For this, we simply used our ideal way [i.e.: personal preference — which is hardly unbreakable law!] to handle the changing "props" of the three establishments. But there are two other ways we thought of which are just as feasible: [A] Use three-faced cutouts attached at the edges (from overhead, they would look like equilateral triangles), each on its own turntable at either end of the table-surface, and rotate each pair into view *horizontally* (this leaves much more room

under the table, too, for the stagehand who puts the gloves and balding-wig onto JUNIOR — or for the BARTENDER to get into position for his rise-into-view — or for JUNIOR to crawl out in the final scene prior to his re-entrance through the draped archway, etc.); likewise, the drapes masking the archway-exit need *not* go all the way to the floor — cut off at 30 inches from the floor, the gap beneath will still be invisible to the audience, and the space there, of course, will permit performers to enter-or-exit beneath it without telltale rippling of the portion the audience can see. [B] Use the three-faced cutouts *without* turntables — however, since they must now be turned by someone onstage — and since we don't want to "kill the suspension-of-disbelief" by having players drop out of character to move them — you will have to have a quick *blackout* between each scene — which is why this method is our least favorite; done as we have outlined the mechanics (via rotating tabletop *or* rotating horizontal turntables), one scene can flow into another just like "dissolves" in movies, with uninterrupted smoothness, and no thumb-twiddling delays in the pacing of each act.

4) MAKEUP: The references in the "Give Him Credit" song to GRETCHEN's fuzzy upper lip should *not* be actually *true*, nor, indeed, *any* such descriptions of her unattractiveness — all she really is is fat-*padded* under her dress so she resembles a walking tepee with arms — until her final entrance in the last act, when she is in a dress (of the same material as the tepee-version, of course) that shows off her actually-quite-excellent form. Same cavil goes for the hangover-look on the three ladies in the final act — they should do this by facial expression, not makeup, because there's no chance to *re*-makeup any of them save GRETCHEN, and we want them all looking their loveliest for the finale.

THE AUTHORS